THE
BULGARIAN
AMERICANS

Senior Consulting Editor

Senator Daniel Patrick Moynihan

Consulting Editors

Ann Orlov
Managing Editor, Harvard
Encyclopedia of American
Ethnic Groups

M. Mark Stolarik
*President, The Balch Institute
for Ethnic Studies, Philadelphia*

James F. Watts
*Chairman, History Department,
City College of New York*

THE
BULGARIAN
AMERICANS

Claudia Carlson
and
David Allen

CHELSEA HOUSE PUBLISHERS
New York   Philadelphia

On the cover: A priest and parishioners at St. Clement Ohridsky Bulgarian Orthodox Church in Detroit in 1942.

CHELSEA HOUSE PUBLISHERS
Editor-in-Chief: Nancy Toff
Executive Editor: Remmel T. Nunn
Managing Editor: Karyn Gullen Browne
Copy Chief: Juliann Barbato
Picture Editor: Adrian G. Allen
Art Director: Maria Epes
Manufacturing Manager: Gerald Levine
Systems Manager: Rachel Vigier

The Peoples of North America
Senior Editor: Sean Dolan

Staff for THE BULGARIAN AMERICANS
Assistant Editor: Elise Donner
Copy Editor: Michael Goodman
Deputy Copy Chief: Mark Rifkin
Picture Research: PAR/NYC
Assistant Art Director: Loraine Machlin
Senior Designer: Noreen M. Lamb
Production Manager: Joseph Romano
Production Coordinator: Marie Claire Cebrián
Cover Illustration: Paul Biniasz
Banner Design: Hrana Janto

First Printing

1   3   5   7   9   8   6   4   2

Library of Congress Cataloging-in-Publication Data
Carlson, Claudia
  The Bulgarian Americans/Claudia Carlson and David Allen.
    p. cm.—(Peoples of North America)
  Includes bibliographical references.
  Summary: Discusses the history, culture, and religion of the Bulgarians, factors encouraging their emigration, and their acceptance as an ethnic group in North America.
  1. Bulgarian Americans—Juvenile literature. [1. Bulgarian Americans.] I. Allen, David J. II. Title. III. Series.
E184.B8C37 1990
973'.0491811—dc20   89-71238
ISBN 0-87754-865-X   CIP
      0-7910-0282-9 (pbk.)   AC

CONTENTS

THE PEOPLES OF NORTH AMERICA

CHELSEA HOUSE PUBLISHERS

A NATION
OF NATIONS

Daniel Patrick Moynihan

The Constitution of the United States begins: "We the People of the United States . . . " Yet, as we know, the United States is not made up of a single group of people. It is made up of many peoples. Immigrants from Europe, Asia, Africa, and Central and South America settled in North America seeking a new life filled with opportunities unavailable in their homeland. Coming from many nations, they forged one nation and made it their own. More than 100 years ago, Walt Whitman expressed this perception of America as a melting pot: "Here is not merely a nation, but a teeming Nation of nations."

Although the ingenuity and acts of courage of these immigrants, our ancestors, shaped the North American way of life, we sometimes take their contributions for granted. This fine series, *The Peoples of North America*, examines the experiences and contributions of the immigrants and how these contributions determined the future of the United States and Canada.

Immigrants did not abandon their ethnic traditions when they reached the shores of North America. Each ethnic group had its own customs and traditions, and each brought different experiences, accomplishments, skills, values, styles of dress, and tastes in food that lingered long after its arrival. Yet this profusion of differences created a singularity, or bond, among the immigrants.

The United States and Canada are unusual in this respect. Whereas religious and ethnic differences have sparked intolerance throughout the rest of the world—from the 17th-century religious wars to the 19th-century nationalist movements in Europe to the near extermination of the Jewish people under Nazi Germany— North Americans have struggled to learn how to respect each other's differences and live in harmony.

Millions of immigrants from scores of homelands brought diversity to our continent. In a mass migration, some 12 million immigrants passed through the waiting rooms of New York's Ellis Island; thousands more came to the West Coast. At first, these immigrants were welcomed because labor was needed to meet the demands of the Industrial Age. Soon, however, the new immigrants faced the prejudice of earlier immigrants who saw them as a burden on the economy. Legislation was passed to limit immigration. The Chinese Exclusion Act of 1882 was among the first laws closing the doors to the promise of America. The Japanese were also effectively excluded by this law. In 1924, Congress set immigration quotas on a country-by-country basis.

Such prejudices might have triggered war, as they did in Europe, but North Americans chose negotiation and compromise instead. This determination to resolve differences peacefully has been the hallmark of the peoples of North America.

The remarkable ability of Americans to live together as one people was seriously threatened by the issue of slavery. It was a symptom of growing intolerance in the world. Thousands of settlers from the British Isles had arrived in the colonies as indentured servants, agreeing to work for a specified number of years on farms or as apprentices in return for passage to America and room and board. When the first Africans arrived in the then-British colonies during the 17th century, some colonists thought that they too should be treated as indentured servants. Eventually, the question of whether the Africans should be viewed as indentured, like the English, or as slaves who could be owned for life, was considered in a Maryland court. The court's calamitous decree held that blacks were slaves bound to lifelong servitude, and so were their children. America went through a time of moral examination and civil war before it finally freed African slaves and their descendants. The principle that all people are created equal had faced its greatest challenge and survived.

Yet the court ruling that set blacks apart from other races fanned flames of discrimination that burned long after slavery was abolished—and that still flicker today. The concept of racism had existed for centuries in countries throughout the world. For instance, when the Manchus conquered China in the 13th century, they decreed that Chinese and Manchus could not intermarry. To impress their superiority on the conquered Chinese, the Manchus ordered all Chinese men to wear their hair in a long braid called a queue.

By the 19th century, some intellectuals took up the banner of racism, citing Charles Darwin. Darwin's scientific studies hypothesized that highly evolved animals were dominant over other animals. Some advocates of this theory applied it to humans, asserting that certain races were more highly evolved than others and thus were superior.

This philosophy served as the basis for a new form of discrimination, not only against nonwhite people but also against various ethnic groups. Asians faced harsh discrimination and were depicted by popular 19th-century newspaper cartoonists as depraved, degenerate, and deficient in intelligence. When the Irish flooded American cities to escape the famine in Ireland, the cartoonists caricatured the typical "Paddy" (a common term for Irish immigrants) as an apelike creature with jutting jaw and sloping forehead.

By the 20th century, racism and ethnic prejudice had given rise to virulent theories of a Northern European master race. When Adolf Hitler came to power in Germany in 1933, he popularized the notion of Aryan supremacy. *Aryan*, a term referring to the Indo-European races, was applied to so-called superior physical characteristics such as blond hair, blue eyes, and delicate facial features. Anyone with darker and heavier features was considered inferior.

Buttressed by these theories, the German Nazi state from 1933 to 1945 set out to destroy European Jews, along with Poles, Russians, and other groups considered inferior. It nearly succeeded. Millions of these people were exterminated.

The tragedies brought on by ethnic and racial intolerance throughout the world demonstrate the importance of North America's efforts to create a society free of prejudice and inequality.

A relatively recent example of the New World's desire to resolve ethnic friction nonviolently is the solution the Canadians found to a conflict between two ethnic groups. A long-standing dispute as to whether Canadian culture was properly English or French resurfaced in the mid-1960s, dividing the peoples of the French-speaking Quebec Province from those of the English-speaking provinces. Relations grew tense, then bitter, then violent. The Royal Commission on Bilingualism and Biculturalism was established to study the growing crisis and to propose measures to ease the tensions. As a result of the commission's recommendations, all official documents and statements from the national government's capital at Ottawa are now issued in both French and English, and bilingual education is encouraged.

The year 1980 marked a coming of age for the United States's ethnic heritage. For the first time, the U.S. Census asked people about their ethnic background. Americans chose from more than 100 groups, including French Basque, Spanish Basque, French Canadian, Afro-American, Peruvian, Armenian, Chinese, and Japanese. The ethnic group with the largest response was English (49.6 million). More than 100 million Americans claimed ancestors from the British Isles, which includes England, Ireland, Wales, and Scotland. There were almost as many Germans (49.2 million) as English. The Irish-American population (40.2 million) was third, but the next largest ethnic group, the Afro-Americans, was a distant fourth (21 million). There was a sizable group of French ancestry (13 million), as well as of Italian (12 million). Poles, Dutch, Swedes, Norwegians, and Russians followed. These groups, and other smaller ones, represent the wondrous profusion of ethnic influences in North America.

Canada, too, has learned more about the diversity of its population. Studies conducted during the French/English conflict showed that Canadians were descended from Ukrainians, Germans, Italians, Chinese, Japanese, native Indians, and Eskimos, among others. Canada found it had no ethnic majority, although nearly half of its immigrant population had come from the British Isles. Canada, like the United States, is a land of immigrants for whom mutual tolerance is a matter of reason as well as principle.

The people of North America are the descendants of one of the greatest migrations in history. And that migration is not over. Koreans, Vietnamese, Nicaraguans, Cubans, and many others are heading for the shores of North America in large numbers. This mix of cultures shapes every aspect of our lives. To understand ourselves, we must know something about our diverse ethnic ancestry. Nothing so defines the North American nations as the motto on the Great Seal of the United States: *E Pluribus Unum*—Out of Many, One.

Darina and Jordan Zekov welcome their daughters Nikolina (left) and Christina (right) to America on June 7, 1986. The children were separated from their parents when the Zekovs, opponents of Bulgaria's Communist government, defected to the West in 1983. A great number of the Bulgarian refugees who have come to the United States since World War II have been political refugees.

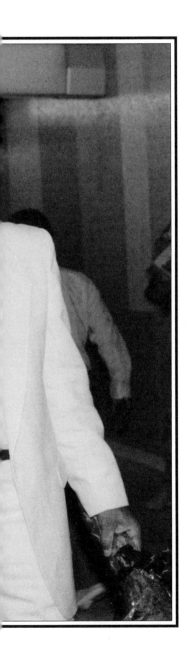

LAND OF MOUNTAINS AND ROSES

Bulgaria is a small country located in the eastern central part of the Balkan Peninsula in southeastern Europe. With an area of 42,823 square miles, it is about the same size as the state of Tennessee, with approximately twice the number of people. From 1880 to 1983, the population of Bulgaria grew from 2,008,000 to 9,150,000, an increase attributable both to natural growth and territorial changes. In 1983, 41 percent of its population lived in rural areas, 59 percent in urban centers. Its capital, Sofia, had a population of 1,047,900 in 1979. Ninety percent of the population is ethnic Bulgarian. Turks form the largest minority group, composing not quite 10 percent of the population, with Gypsies, Armenians, Russians, and Greeks constituting smaller minorities. Nearly 90 percent of Bulgarians belong to the autonomous Bulgarian Orthodox church. Muslims make up the only significant religious minority at 8.6 percent; a small number of people are Roman Catholic, Protestant, or Jewish.

Bulgaria borders on Romania, across the Danube River, in the north; on Greece and Turkey in the south; on Yugoslavia in the west; and on 154 miles of Black Sea coast in the east. Bulgaria is a mountainous country; its dominant topographic features are the Balkan Mountains and the Danubian plain in the north and the

Rhodope Mountains and the Maritsa plain in the south. The Danubian plain is Bulgaria's primary agricultural region; the Maritsa plain too is very fertile and is planted with wheat, corn, tobacco, rice, sunflowers, herbs, and mulberry trees. The Tundzha Valley is renowned for its natural beauty and for its profusion of roses; from these flowers is extracted attar of roses, an oil vital in making perfume. Because of its beaches and its abundance of mineral springs, valued since the time of the Roman Empire for their healing properties, Bulgaria is a favorite holiday destination for Eastern bloc tourists. The most popular resort area is in and around Varna, near the shores of the Black Sea.

The climate of Bulgaria varies widely by region and topography. Mountainous areas are known for severe winters and cool summers. Southern areas feature generally warmer temperatures year-round. Lowlands experience occasional droughts; higher elevations have high annual precipitation. Forests cover one-third of the land; bear, wild boar, elk, wolves, chamois (a small goatlike antelope), and wildcats inhabit the forested regions.

Bulgarians Abroad

Despite its resources, Bulgaria has often found itself unable to support its population. In the early years of the 20th century, thousands of Bulgarians left home for economic reasons. Between 1880 and 1905, the Bulgarian population increased by 50 percent, largely because of the introduction of better sanitation and public health programs. At about the same time, the Bulgarian government determined to build a modern state by, among other things, modernizing the nation's army, schools, and railroads. Unfortunately, as there were few industries (only 35 in 1887) or wealthy citizens to finance these improvements with their tax money, the burden of payment fell on the peasantry, which then constituted the vast majority of the Bulgarian population. With land already scarce because of the population increase and their tax obligations increasing, many Bulgarians

began considering emigrating to the United States, where industrialization had created hundreds of thousands of jobs.

The need for cheap labor in the United States and the relative availability of steamship and railway travel enabled many Bulgarians to leave their farms and villages. Between 1900 and 1910, approximately 50,000 Bulgarians and Macedonian Bulgarians, most of them unmarried peasant men, immigrated to the United States, where they settled in the steel and mining towns and industrial centers of the Midwest and Northeast.

Some 1,700 Bulgarian immigrants made their way to Canada during that same time; 60 percent of those settled in Ontario.

The Macedonian-Bulgarian immigrants had political as well as economic reasons for seeking a new homeland. (Inhabited in part by ethnic Bulgarians, the region of Macedonia was at the time a frequent object of dispute between Turkey, Greece, Bulgaria, and Serbia, a Slavic state that would eventually become part of Yugoslavia.) The failed 1903 Ilinden or St. Ilya's Day uprising, in which Macedonians had tried to win their freedom from the Turks, resulted in the massacre of 5,000 Macedonian revolutionaries and villagers. Turkish armies destroyed three Macedonian provinces, leaving 100,000 people homeless. Some 30,000 Macedonians fled across the border to Bulgaria, where within months the greatest wave of Bulgarian and Macedonian emigration was under way.

About 60 percent of the Bulgarian immigrants who came to North America in the years before World War I were from Macedonia, with the largest number coming from the provinces hardest hit by Turkish reprisals. Most of these —80 percent—were peasants; the other 20 percent were craftsmen, laborers, and intellectuals. Those Bulgarian immigrants who hailed from Macedonia, as opposed to those who hailed from "the kingdom," or the independent Bulgarian state, referred to themselves as Macedonians only in the sense of identifying with a geographic area. In terms of nationality or ethnic descent, they considered themselves Bulgarian. Since 1918, Macedonia has been divided among Bulgaria, Greece, and the Yugoslavian state, each of which has based its claim to the land on ethnic, linguistic, historical, and racial arguments. Race is a poor foundation for such claims, for according to Nikolay G. Altankov, author of *The Bulgarian-Americans*, there is "no consensus as to the racial origin of the inhabitants of Macedonia." Altankov adds that most of the Macedonians in the United States identify with Bulgarian culture and history. Since 1945, the majority of Macedonians who have come to this country began their journey in areas controlled by Yugoslavia and Greece. In the late 1940s, when Greece attempted to drive the Macedonians from their native land, approximately 70,000 emigrated overseas, many of them to the United States. Yugoslavian statistics indicate that between 1960 and 1977, 40,000 Macedonians emigrated to the United States, Canada, and Australia. Some were political dissidents, but the majority left in search of economic opportunity.

Because of their relatively small numbers, the Bulgarian and Macedonian-Bulgarian immigrants who arrived in the United States before World War I tended to settle near other recently arrived Slavic immigrants, such as the Serbs, who shared similar cultural backgrounds and values. Eastern European immigrants clustered in the ethnic enclaves of such midwestern cities as Granite City and Madison, Illinois, which in 1907 had a combined total of 6,000 Bulgarian-American residents. Most of these immigrants arrived with little or no money and few marketable skills; as a result they had no choice but to accept low-paying unskilled jobs in mines and factories. Poverty and squalor defined most of the urban neighborhoods inhabited by Bulgarian immigrants, but the typical new arrival was not interested in luxury; most had come to America with the intention of returning home as soon as they could make enough money to buy a better life in Bulgaria. Between 1910 and 1929, the number of returnees exceeded the number of new immigrants. Some went home to buy a new farm or business; others returned to serve in the Bulgarian army during the Balkan Wars.

In 1924, the United States passed the National Origins or the Johnson-Reid Immigration Act, which instituted a quota system based on national origins designed to favor people from northern and western Europe whose coming would not significantly change the ethnic composition of American society. The act

Bulgarian peasant women take a break from picking roses in Kanzanlik in 1928. For generations, the lack of economic opportunity had forced many peasants to seek work abroad.

restricted the number of Bulgarians allowed to enter the United States to only 100 a year. (In 1965, the Hart-Celler Act lifted the national origins quota restrictions.) Official immigration records show that only 7,660 Bulgarians were admitted to the United States between 1924 and 1965, but the actual figure is thought to be much higher, because during these decades thousands of people of all nationalities entered the United States illegally, either through Canada or Mexico. Other Bulgarians may have entered with Turkish, Greek, Serbian, Romanian, or Yugoslavian passports, since many immigrants were recorded under the country of their last residence, rather than by the country of their birth. Still other Bulgarians went unrecorded because for a time, U.S. immigration statistics classified Bulgarians with Serbs and Montenegrins. Even so, it is reasonable to assume that today there are only about 70,000 Bulgarian immigrants and their descendants in America.

Between the two world wars, the majority of Bulgarian and Macedonian-Bulgarian immigrants were women and children joining husbands and fathers who had decided to make their home in America. Since the end of World War II, when Bulgaria became a Communist state, the Bulgarians who left their native country have been primarily political refugees and professionals seeking intellectual freedom. Although the Bulgarian government has periodically made it difficult if not impossible to emigrate, thousands of its citizens have managed to escape to the West. It remains to be seen how the easing of tensions between the East and the West that took place at the end of the 1980s will affect Bulgarian immigration to the United States.

ТНѢ ЕЦѢ, НСѢ НГНАЛѢ ПРѢ БЫВААШЕ·
ЦѢ ѢЖ ЕЛНХ АНЛАВѢ ЗНЕНАВНДѢ ВѢ ЫАКО
ПНАННЦ ЖНВ НН ОПНИЦ Х · НО ГРАННХѢ
ОЛ ЖША САНПОЗОРЫ ДѢ ЖЦА · ВѢ Х ТРОБѢ
Ѣ ЛОУ ВѢ НЗНАЛЕТ Ь · НВ ЛАСТ Ь ВѢСХЫТН
ПРѢ ЖД ЕВ РѢ АЛ ЕНЕН ПРѢ ЖД ЕГ О ЛА ·

Ѣ НАБ НЕ ФОТЇА НЗ ГНА Ѿ ЦРК ВЕ · НП Л
КЫ СѠД АСТ Ь ПРѢ СТОЛ Ь НГ НАГ НЕВН·
ВѢ ХОТѢ В Ь Ж ЕН НА РО ДОУ НЛ ѢН НЕ СѠ
ДАТН · НН ЗЫ СКА ВѢ ДО Л АКЫ ЗЛАТО
Х РАНАЦ ХА · НЖ ЕПРѢ ВѢ Е СѢ Т А ЗА АХ Ѫ

FROM GOLDEN AGE
TO SOCIALIST STATE

The Bulgars are a people of central Asian origin. During the 5th century A.D., they founded states along the northern shores of the Black Sea, particularly in the northern Crimea. In A.D. 679, the Utiguri-Bulgarian tribe crossed the Danube, conquered the local Slavs, and established the first Bulgarian kingdom in the region of present-day Bulgaria. The militarized Bulgar tribe gave its name to the new state but was otherwise assimilated into the indigenous Slavic population. Over the following three centuries, the minority Bulgar population adopted both the Slavic language and customs; the society it helped create reflected elements of both the Slavic agricultural community and the Bulgars' military structure. Throughout the 7th and 8th centuries, the Bulgars waged war against Slavic groups and Byzantium; during the reign of Krum, who ruled from 802 to 814, Bulgaria became a unified state, strong enough to pose a threat to Byzantium's independence. Krum's successor, Omortag, extended the Bulgarian kingdom; Omortag's son Malamir consolidated the new state and resisted the spread of Christianity.

Christianity and the Golden Age

The first Bulgarian kingdom lasted from A.D. 679 to 1018, a period that witnessed the flowering of a distinctly Bulgarian culture enlivened by Turkish, Byzantine, and Slavic influence. The majority of the people in Bulgarian society were serfs, landless peasants who labored for the landowning *boyars*. The boyars, or higher nobility, were vassals of the king who supported or opposed him as they saw fit; between them and the serfs were the *bagains*, or lower nobility.

Christianity was introduced in 865 during the reign of Czar Boris I. Although legend relates that Boris was frightened into accepting baptism by the ghastly pictures of hell a monk painted on his palace walls, Boris more likely saw conversion as a politically wise choice, a decision that would ease his relations with his powerful neighbor, the Byzantine Empire.

At the time, the Christian church was divided into two rival factions, the Roman Catholic church, led by the pope in Rome, and the Eastern Orthodox church, led by a patriarch in Constantinople. Boris carefully considered which branch of the Christian church it would be most advantageous to join. He agreed with the Byzantine missionaries St. Cyril and St. Methodius that church services should be said in the vernacular, or the language of the Bulgar people. The Roman Catholic bishops disagreed and insisted that Hebrew, Greek, and Latin were the only languages appropriate for communicating the Word of God. Boris also wanted the Bulgarian church to to be able to exercise its independence by choosing its own clergy, and most significantly, by electing its own patriarch. When the pope refused to allow the Bulgarians this ecclesiastical power, Boris decided to ally the Bulgarian church with the Eastern Orthodox church, which was willing to accept his terms. In A.D. 870, Constantinople formally recognized the independence of the Bulgarian church. Over the subsequent centuries, the Bulgarians managed to

This illumination from the Chronicle of Manasses, *a 14th-century Slavonic manuscript, shows the defeat of the Bulgarian king Samuel in 1014 by the Byzantine emperor Basil II, the dreaded "Slayer of the Bulgarians," who took 15,000 Bulgarian soldiers prisoner and blinded all but 1 out of every 100. The soldiers who retained their sight led their mutilated countrymen back to Samuel, who supposedly died of grief at their awful plight.*

maintain their church and remained fiercely loyal to their faith.

Following the establishment of the Bulgarian church, the missionaries Kliment and Naum, followers of St. Cyril and St. Methodius, settled in Bulgaria, where they translated important passages from the Bible and Byzantine religious texts into Old Church Slavonic (Old Bulgarian), using the alphabet St. Cyril had created based on the spoken Slavic language. The Cyrillic alphabet is still used in Bulgaria. At first, the Cyrillic alphabet was only used for translating Scripture; later, the Bulgarians began to use it for all scholarship and literature.

Between 893 and 927, during the reign of Simeon, the self-proclaimed "Czar of the Bulgarians and Greeks," Bulgaria expanded its borders, and the city of Sofia became a center for art, architecture, literature, trade, and education. The frescoes on church and monastery walls that survive from this golden age are considered masterpieces of Byzantine art, and it was during this period that Slavic legal codes were most likely first compiled.

A Weakening Kingdom

Unlike his father, Simeon's son Peter was uninterested in military conquests; during his reign Bulgaria was invaded by the Russian Svyatoslav I, grand prince of Kiev, and the Macedonian Slavs staged several rebellions. The country was torn internally by the Bogomil heresy, a religious and social movement that preached pacifism, equality, and disobedience to an abusive authority. In order to protect his territory, Byzantine emperor John I Zimisces attacked Prince Svyatoslav, who had made himself master of Bulgaria; in 972, the emperor defeated the prince, abolished the Bulgarian patriarchate, and declared Bulgaria a Byzantine province. Their declarations notwithstanding, the Byzantines exercised rule only in eastern Bulgaria. Between 980 and 1014, the western regions were consolidated by Samuel, a Bulgarian noble, but in 1014 the bloodthirsty Byzantine emperor Basil II defeated Samuel's army, sealing his triumph by blinding almost 15,000 Bulgarian soldiers. From 1018 until 1185, Bulgaria and Macedonia were ruled by a Byzantine imperial governor who interfered little with local institutions. Nevertheless, most Bulgarians existed in poverty and misery, and a large number were drawn to Bogomilism.

In the 12th century, the Byzantine Empire began to decline in power, and with the help of the Magyar, Serbian, and Norman armies, the Bulgarians seized Sofia. In 1186, the Bulgarians overthrew their Byzantine rulers; in 1187, the Byzantine Empire signed a treaty with Bulgaria and formally recognized its independence. Two brothers of the Bulgarian nobility, Peter and Ivan Asen I, were the first corulers of the second Bulgarian kingdom, which lasted until 1396. Under Ivan Asen II, who reigned from 1218 to 1241, Bulgaria prospered. Its domestic and foreign trade increased; architecture, religious literature, and the arts flourished; harmonious relations between the nobility and the monasteries prevailed; and the frontier was expanded. Ivan Asen II died during the Tatar invasion of the Balkans, as a result of which the Bulgars were compelled to pay an annual tribute to the nomadic Turkic conquerors. For the next century, the Bulgarian kingdom continued to decline as the result of a combination of

These 16th-century books were displayed in 1980 at the book depository of the Rila Monastery, located in the heart of the Rila Dagh Mountains in southwestern Bulgaria. Along with the Hilendar and the Zegraf monasteries, the Rila Monastery has always been a symbol of patriotism and learning.

internal stresses, including a proliferation of religious sects associated with Bogomilism, and external threats, in the form of repeated invasions by the Magyars.

Five Centuries of Turkish Rule

The greatest threat to Bulgarian self-determination came from the Ottoman Turks, who conquered Bulgaria in the last decade of the 14th century. Turkish rule was oppressive and often brutal; many Bulgarians fled to Russia, Serbia, Romania, and elsewhere in order to escape forced conversion to Islam and economic exploitation. Not long after their victory over Bulgaria and Macedonia, Turkish armies conquered Greece and Serbia, giving the Ottoman Empire control over the entire Balkan Peninsula.

The Turks set out to wring tribute from their conquered domains and to spread the Islamic faith. Acting in the name of Allah, Turkish soldiers desecrated and destroyed the beautiful frescoes, books, churches, and monasteries that were the products of the Bulgarian golden age. Fortunately, Bulgarian priests were able to preserve some samples of national literature in secluded monasteries. For the majority of the people, their spoken language, their Christian faith, and their folk crafts and folk songs were all that remained untouched. Centuries of economic and cultural development were undone in only a few decades of Turkish rule.

When the Ottoman Empire was strong, the Bulgarian peasant's situation was tolerable. At times, daily life was no worse than it had been under the feudal system of the boyars. Within limits, the people were allowed to practice local self-government, attend their churches, and speak their language among themselves. However, in the 18th and 19th centuries, when the Ottoman Empire began to weaken under the pressure of dynastic quarrels and other internal struggles, the Turkish army reacted by persecuting Bulgaria's Christian population, which it charged with encouraging and abetting outside invaders, such as the Russians. Turkish reprisals were uniformly brutal.

The Turkish government also used political restructuring to control the Bulgarian population. They renamed the Balkan Peninsula "Rumili" and subdivided it into administrative divisions effectively ruled by lesser Turkish officials. Each local administrator was responsible to his superior in a system of accountability that ended with the sultan. This many-layered system resulted in the peasants paying, through taxation, for the corruption and excesses of an entire population of Turkish officials.

To most Bulgarians, religious persecution was perhaps the most onerous aspect of their subjugation. The Turks levied additional taxes on Christians. The boyars were forced to convert to Islam and follow Turkish customs or lose their wealth and authority. Most boyars chose to remain Christian and live in their villages as farmers, effectively renouncing their position as the traditional ruling class. They received none of the privileges, such as lower taxes, that were given to converts to Islam. The widespread refusal of the Bulgarian populace to convert to Islam emphasized the intimate connection between Bulgarian nationalism and the Bulgarian Orthodox church.

Greek Interference in the Bulgarian Church

The nationalism rooted in the Bulgarian Orthodox church posed a substantial challenge to Turkish rule. The sultan met this threat by formally recognizing the Greek patriarch in Constantinople as the sole ecclesiastic representative of Christians in the Ottoman Empire, thus reducing the Bulgarian church to a mere sub-patriarchate within the Greek Orthodox church. Mass was said in Greek, confessions were heard through an interpreter, and religious texts written in the Bulgarian language were burned. Bulgarian schoolchildren were forced to learn and recite their lessons in Greek.

Although elements of both Turkish and Byzantine architectural and decorative styles contributed to the appearance of Bulgarian Orthodox churches, the Bulgarian church has become an emblem of Bulgaria's national identity and independence.

In the early 1760s, Father Paisii Hilendnarski, a monk from the monastery of Hilendar on Mount Athos, inspired a revival of nationalistic pride. Father Paisii had read extensively about the old Bulgarian church and empire in the well-stocked library of his monastery and became concerned that the rich Bulgarian cultural heritage was being neglected. In 1762, he issued *A Slavonic-Bulgarian History of the Peoples, Tsars and Saints, and of all their Deeds and of the Bulgarian Way of Life*, a book intended to warn his fellow Bulgarians about the dangers of Hellenism (Greek influence) and to remind his compatriots that there was good reason to be proud of the homeland:

Of all the Slav peoples the most glorious were the Bulgarians; they were the first who called themselves kings, the first to have a Patriarch, the first to adopt the Christian faith, and they it was who conquered the largest amount of territory. Thus of all the Slav peoples they were the strongest and the most honoured, and the first Slav saints cast their radiance from among the Bulgarian people and through the Bulgarian language.

The monk's book did not start a revolution, but it did help promote education and learning in the Bulgarian language, and with renewed cultural pride came increased political awareness. With the Bulgarian educated classes united in demanding increased cultural freedom, in 1835 the Turks were forced to allow the establishment of Bulgarian schools. By the 1850s, most large communities had built schools in which the Bulgarian language was taught. By 1878, the year in which Bulgaria finally obtained its independence from the Ottoman Empire, 2,000 schools in Bulgaria offered a free education in the nation's native tongue. The most promising students were often sent to continue their studies in France, Austria, Russia, Turkey, and England. Those who returned often became teachers and devoted themselves to providing education to the peasantry.

In the second half of the 19th century, an interest in folklore as a reflection of the life and culture of the peasantry, who still constituted the majority of the Bulgarian population, developed among the intelligentsia. Dimitar Miladionov, a Macedonian-born professor, traveled with his brother throughout Macedonia collecting folk songs, legends, proverbs, and riddles from the peasantry, as well as compiling accounts of their daily life. The brothers were forced to go about their work secretly so as not to be discovered by the Turkish authorities or the Greek clergy. Unable to find a publisher in Russia, in 1861 they were financed by a Croatian Roman Catholic bishop, Josip J. Strossmayer, a major advocate of southern Slavic unity. The publication of the Miladionovs' collection documented the successful struggle of the Bulgarian populace to maintain their indigenous folk culture despite Turkish and Greek repression. Recognizing that the Miladionovs' work would indeed spur Bulgarian nationalism, the Greek clergy had the brothers imprisoned in Istanbul (formerly Constantinople), where they died in 1862.

The Rise of Nationalism

Bulgaria was greatly influenced by the various democratic movements that took place in western Europe in the late 1700s and early to mid-1800s. To the long-suffering Bulgarian populace, the French Revolution served as a particularly potent example of an oppressed people overthrowing its tyrannical leaders. Protestant and Roman Catholic missionaries in Bulgaria sent promising students to western universities in Paris, London, and Vienna, where they learned about the greater political, personal, and economic freedoms enjoyed by citizens of France, Britain, and Austria. Such knowledge strengthened the Bulgarian determination to oppose Ottoman rule, as did an example from closer to home. In 1830, aided by Bulgarian soldiers, Greece won its independence from the Turks. Weakened by internal political corruption and wars with Russia and Austria-Hungary, preoccupied with British and French provocation in Egypt and the Levant, the Ottoman Empire found itself bedeviled within Bulgaria by the frequent revolts of the *hayduti*, armed brigands who over time would take on a Robin Hood–like aura in Bulgarian lore.

Yielding to pressure, in 1870 the Turks allowed the Bulgarian clergy to reestablish a Bulgarian national church under its own exarch, an ecclesiastical rank second only to a patriarch and one high enough to indicate a truly separate church. The reinstatement of their church gave Bulgarians high hopes concerning their independence.

Russian Liberation of Bulgaria and Macedonia

One year before the Bulgarian church regained its independence, Bulgarian nationalists in exile had formed the Bulgarian Central Revolutionary Committee in Bucharest, Romania. By 1875, the group had helped organize uprisings in Bosnia and Herzegovina, Slavic regions where many Bulgarians had settled. In the spring of 1876, with the Ottoman Empire preoccupied with the unrest in Bosnia and with the prospect of war with newly independent Serbia, Georgi Benkovski and fellow members of the Bulgarian Central Revolutionary Committee led a revolt against Turkish rule in Bulgaria. Although the revolt, known as the April Uprising, failed to liberate the Bulgarians, or even to gather much popular support, the Turkish reprisals were so brutal that they outraged Europe.

Januarius Aloysius MacGahan, a young American journalist, was assigned in 1876 by the London *Daily News* to investigate reports of atrocities by Turkish irregular troops against unarmed Bulgarian peasants. His previous experience traveling in Europe and Russia as a war correspondent had prepared him well for the Balkan assignment. MacGahan's articles describing the horrors he witnessed created a furor throughout Europe and helped to convince the Russian leader, Czar Alexander II, of the necessity of mounting an invasion of Bulgaria in order to free his fellow Slavs from the hated Turks.

On August 2, 1876, MacGahan entered the ruins of the town of Batak, where 7,800 of the 9,000 inhabitants had been murdered by Turkish irregular troops known as *bashi-bazooks*. MacGahan described his ride past heaps of skulls and scattered bones scavenged by wild dogs and his arrival at the village church, which had been set on fire with hundreds of people trapped inside:

> What we saw there was too frightful for more than a hasty glance.... An immense number of bodies had been partly burned there and the charred and

"The Liberator of the Bulgarian People," Januarius MacGahan, shown here in a photo taken around 1873, began his career in journalism as a special correspondent for the New York Herald *during the Franco-Prussian War. MacGahan received his honorific appellation for the role his reporting played in helping Bulgaria obtain its independence.*

blackened remains that seemed to fill up halfway to the low, dark arches, and make them lower and darker, were still lying in a state of putrefaction too frightful to look upon.

MacGahan's articles and British statesman William Gladstone's forceful condemnation of the brutality helped turn international public opinion against the Turks. As the self-proclaimed protector of its little "Slavic Brother" in the Balkans, Russia was particularly outraged over the Turkish brutality. Leaders in Western Europe had been afraid of speaking out against the Turks because they feared increased Russian influence in the Balkans, but the public outcry against the Turks finally forced them to break their silence. Diplomatic demands from Britain, France, Germany, Austria, and Russia forced the Ottoman Empire to promise reforms. The Russian government insisted on the right to inspect Turkish-held lands for compliance; when the sultan refused to grant this right, Alexander II declared war on the Ottoman Empire in the summer of 1877. Less than a year later, the Russians proclaimed the freedom of Bulgaria and Macedonia; the Turks agreed to grant Bulgaria and most of Macedonia their autonomy by virtue of the Treaty of San Stefano, which was signed on

This print, made from an eyewitness drawing of 1878, depicts the army of the Russian czar, Alexander II, as it prepares to move on Sofia during the Russian campaign to free the Balkan states from Turkish rule.

March 3, 1878. But, still fearful of Russia's influence in the Balkans, the other major European powers forced the undoing of the San Stefano agreement. At the Congress of Berlin, which took place in the summer of 1878, Bulgaria was partitioned. It was decided that Bulgaria proper was to be limited to the area between the Danube River and the Balkan Mountains; the area to the south was declared an autonomous province to be called Eastern Rumelia. Macedonia was to revert entirely to Turkish rule.

On February 22, 1879, the Bulgarian constitutional assembly convened and wrote what was considered one of the most progressive constitutions of its time. It provided for a prince as head of state, a unicameral legislature, called the Subranie, elected by limited male suffrage, and personal liberties including freedom of religion, of the press, and from arbitrary arrest.

Germany's chancellor, Otto von Bismarck (in center of group of three men standing at front), acted as president of the Congress of Berlin in the summer of 1878. Referring to himself as an "honest broker," Bismarck hoped to avoid war between Austria and Russia over territorial settlements in the Balkans, including the disposition of Bulgaria.

Troubles in the New Bulgarian State

Despite the heady feelings that accompanied freedom, during its first few years the autonomous principality of Bulgaria struggled. On April 29, 1879, the constitutional assembly had elected Prince Alexander of Battenberg to the Bulgarian throne. With the support of the Russian government, Alexander suspended the new constitution and pursued conservative policies. The Bulgarian economy suffered from the loss of Turkish

Prince Alexander of Battenberg was elected to the Bulgarian throne on April 29, 1879. His tenure as prince was characterized by conflict created by his own desire to safeguard Russian interests and the efforts of Bulgarian liberals to bring about political and economic reform. The Russians forced Alexander to abdicate in September 1886.

markets, and it staggered under the weight of mismanagement and lack of foreign investment.

In September 1885, Bulgaria announced that it was unifying with Rumelia. This turn of events upset Serbia, which had been planning its own move on the territory; instead, it declared war on Bulgaria, but the Serbian people showed little appetite for battle against their fellow Slavs, and peace was declared in March 1886. Six months later, the conservative government in czarist Russia forced the abdication of Prince Alexander, who had begun to show alarming liberal tendencies. The remaining years of the 19th century in Bulgaria were characterized by political unrest and disputes between Prince Ferdinand of Saxe-Coburg, Alexander's successor, and Stefan Stambulov, Bulgaria's premier, over which direction the country should take in foreign affairs. Ferdinand wished to strengthen Bulgaria's ties with Russia; Stambulov supported closer alliances with western Europe. With the assassination of Stambulov in 1896, the prince's viewpoint prevailed. In 1908, Bulgaria proclaimed itself completely independent, and Ferdinand became its czar.

Macedonia and the Doomed Uprising of 1903

Although Macedonia remained under Turkish rule after the liberation of 1878, its own nationalism found a voice in the Internal Macedonian Revolutionary Organization (IMRO), which was formed in 1893 by Damjan Gruev with the stated goal of obtaining Macedonian independence through revolutionary means.

Ten years later, on August 2, 1903, the IMRO staged the Ilinden or St. Ilya's Day uprising. On that day, 26,000 Macedonian rebels took up arms against the Turks, but in the ensuing battles superior Turkish numbers and firepower won the day. Within three months, the IMRO forces had been defeated. The fighting had left thousands of people dead and 100,000 homeless; 30,000 refugees fled to Bulgaria.

A political cartoon that appeared in a British magazine in November 1912 depicts a new sun rising over a liberated Macedonia. Although Bulgaria had gained its autonomy in 1878, Macedonia remained under Turkish rule until Bulgaria, Serbia, Greece, and Montenegro united in 1912 to end the sway of the Ottoman Empire in eastern Europe.

In 1912, Greece and three Slavic nations—Bulgaria, Serbia, and Montenegro—united to drive the Turks from the Balkans. The first phase of the Balkan Wars ended with Turkey driven from virtually all of its European possessions, but when Greece and Serbia refused to evacuate Macedonia, where much of the fighting had taken place, Bulgaria turned on her two former allies, who were now joined by Romania and Turkey. Bulgaria was unable to stand alone against this quadruple alliance and was forced to cede territory to all four powers. Greece and Serbia divided almost all of Macedonia between them. At the outbreak of World War I in 1914, Bulgaria still coveted Macedonia; when the Central Powers (Germany, Austria-Hungary, and the Ottoman Empire) offered Bulgaria that section of Macedonia under Serbian rule (Serbia fought in the war on the Allied side), Bulgaria cast its lot with them. It invaded Serbia in 1915, but its hopes were dashed with the Allied victory in 1918.

To the Second World War

The interwar years in Bulgaria and Macedonia were characterized by political instability, strikes, inflation, and IMRO terrorism. Control of the Bulgarian government alternated between peasant and bourgeois parties as well as various coalitions, but no group had much success in handling Bulgaria's long-standing economic problems, which were greatly aggravated by the worldwide depression that began in 1929.

All these circumstances helped lead to the formation of Zveno (Link), a political group composed of intellectuals intent upon creating an ideological and political foundation for national unity and reform. On May 19,

An armed Bulgarian guard watches at the border between his own country and Yugoslavia in this 1935 photograph. Throughout its history, Bulgaria has often had to befriend a stronger power in order to protect itself.

1934, Zveno, in league with another organization, the Officers' Club, staged a successful coup d'état and erected an authoritarian government that severely restricted personal and political liberties while aligning itself with Britain and France and opening diplomatic relations with the Soviet Union. The following year, King Boris III regained control of the government and established his own authoritarian state. He then concentrated on furthering ties with the fascist states of Germany and Italy. When World War II erupted in 1939, Bulgaria declared itself neutral, but on March 1, 1941, it formally joined the Axis powers. On December 13 of that same year, Bulgaria declared war on the United States, France, and Britain.

The rural town of Melnik, Bulgaria, 65 miles from the Greek port of Salonika, was occupied by German troops on March 3, 1941. Two days earlier, Bulgaria had formally joined the Axis powers; later that year it would declare war on the United States, France, and Great Britain.

King Boris of Bulgaria (right) shakes the hand of a member of the German air force in Sofia in April 1941. Although the Bulgarian government allied itself with Germany in World War II, Bulgaria did successfully oppose the deportation of its Jewish population.

Alliance with the Nazis meant that Bulgaria was expected to do its share to fulfill the demonic plan of Germany's maniacal dictator, Adolf Hitler, for the extermination of all of Europe's Jews. The Bulgarian government did go so far as to institute several repressive measures against Bulgaria's 50,000 Jews —mandates were issued expelling them from the nation's major cities, some were arrested and placed in internment camps, and an order for deportation was even issued— but the outraged actions of the Bulgarian populace saved the nation's Jewry from delivery to the concentration camps. The Bulgarian Orthodox church pleaded that anti-Jewish measures be eased, powerful Jews argued for their people and bribed officials, and farmers in northern Bulgaria threatened to lie down on the railroad tracks to stop the trains carrying the Jews to the gas chambers. Boris successfully resisted the great pressure exerted on him by the Nazis, and in March 1943 Bulgaria's Jews were released from detention, an event the Bulgarians remember as the "miracle of the Jewish people." (Jews in Macedonia and Thrace, a Greek region occupied by Bulgaria in 1941, were not as fortunate. In 1941, 11,000 Jews from those regions were deported to Hitler's concentration camps.) After the war, some 45,000 Bulgarian Jews emigrated to Israel.

The Communist State

When Boris suddenly died on August 28, 1943, a council of regents, with Germany's approval, took control of the Bulgarian government. Bulgaria's Communists had gained in power during the war years, particularly as a result of the leading role they played in the Fatherland Front, a coalition of resistance groups. When the Soviet Union declared war on Bulgaria and invaded in September 1944, the Communists staged a coup d'état and installed a new government under the leadership of Kimon Georgiev. An armistice was signed in Moscow on October 28, 1944.

In November 1989, a Bulgarian woman signs a petition demanding the release of political prisoners and the institution of democratic reforms. That same month, Todor Zhivkov, head of Bulgaria's repressive regime since the mid-1950s, resigned, raising the hopes of Bulgarians that their country would emulate the democratic reforms then taking place elsewhere in Eastern Europe.

Over the next 45 years, the Bulgarian Communists solidified their control over the government while allying Bulgaria firmly with the countries of the Warsaw Pact, the military and economic alliance of Eastern bloc nations. During that time, Bulgaria was considered to be the Soviet Union's most steadfast ally, and its government, under the leadership of Vulko Chervenko and Todor Zhivkov and aided by the work of its ubiquitous secret police force, was regarded as one of the world's most repressive, presiding over an extremely closed society. Bulgaria also essentially renounced its claims to

Two Bulgarian Turks embrace at a train station near the Bulgarian border on July 4, 1989. The men and the women watching anxiously from the window of a train behind them were among the more than 300,000 Turks who left Bulgaria as a result of the government's forced assimilation and deportation campaign.

hegemony over all of Macedonia, and Bulgarian society was greatly affected by several significant population shifts. Perhaps the most important, in terms of the nation's demographics, have been the emigration of most of Bulgaria's Jews to Israel and the expulsion, in the early 1950s and again in the late 1980s, of a total of more than 460,000 Turks.

In the late 1980s, the Bulgarian government tried to forcibly assimilate the growing Muslim Turkish minority, which despite earlier expulsions accounted for 15 percent of the total population. The Bulgarian government shut down Turkish-language schools and newspapers, fined people for speaking Turkish in public, closed mosques on all days other than religious holidays, and banned circumcision, which is required by Islamic law. Many Turks fled rather than endure such repression; some told of being forced by government authorities to relinquish their family names and adopt Bulgarian ones. Officials in Sofia insist that there are no real Turks in Bulgaria, only Bulgarians who were once forced to convert to Islam under Ottoman rule. By September 1989, 300,000 Turks had left behind their jobs, property, friends, and family in their haste to emigrate; the migration marks one of the greatest population shifts in Europe since World War II.

Like the other Communist nations of Eastern Europe, Bulgaria underwent profound changes in 1989. Encouraged by the movement toward political and economic liberalization in the Soviet Union and in many of the Warsaw Pact countries, Bulgarians took to the streets of Sofia and other cities to protest the repression and economic stagnation of the Zhivkov regime. Faced with massive popular opposition and the unwillingness of the Soviet leader, Mikhail Gorbachev, to support a hard-line position, Zhivkov resigned in November 1989. The government then issued a remarkable acknowledgement of the many "errors" that had been made under the Communist regime, raising the hopes of Bulgarians that a new era of freedom had dawned.

A young Bulgarian peasant girl
carries water from the local well.
Decades into the 20th century,
much of the Bulgarian peasantry
worked their land using methods
and implements similar to those
that they had used for centuries.
The hardship of rural life convinced many Bulgarians to
emigrate to America in the early
decades of the 20th century.

"AMERICAMANIA" AND THE MIGRANT LABORER

The reasons why Bulgarians left their homeland in large numbers in the early 1900s for the great unknown of life in America are rooted in the economic conditions then prevailing in Bulgaria. At the beginning of the 20th century, just before the great wave of Bulgarian emigration, Bulgaria and Macedonia consisted mainly of small villages and individually owned farms. In 1903, when the great wave of Bulgarian emigration began, nearly 80 percent of the population were farmers. Sofia, Bulgaria's capital, had a population of just 90,000.

The average Bulgarian farm was small, measuring between 12 and 30 acres, with most tending to be closer to 12 acres. Farms were usually spread out around the village in several parcels. More than three-quarters of the farmland in Bulgaria was devoted to growing wheat, corn, oats, or rye, either for the farmer's table or for export. The modern method of crop rotation (grow-ing different crops in alternating seasons in order to replenish the soil with various vitamins and minerals) was essentially unknown, as was the use of fertilizer. The Bulgarian farmer still relied on leaving land fallow as his chief means of improving the soil for the next growing season. In 1903, more than 30 percent of Bulgaria's farm acreage lay fallow.

Most villages set aside a portion of common land as grazing ground for oxen and water buffalo, the most common draft animals. Farmers also usually kept pigs and chickens, and sheepherding was practiced in the southern Rhodope Mountains. Although Bulgarian shepherds were discriminated against after the political separation of Bulgaria from Turkey in 1878, they still brought their flocks to the traditional markets of Adrianople and Constantinople.

In addition to the staple crop of wheat, a farmer might raise fodder hay for his animals and small quantities of garden vegetables for his family's meals. He might also tend an orchard or raise bees for honey. Although only about seven percent of all farmland was reserved for these supplementary crops, they provided a valuable addition to the family diet, a hedge against a bad wheat harvest, and a supply for the household's winter needs. Even in good years, most farm families were not well off. The rude dwelling of the typical Bulgarian farmer was described in *Peter Menikoff: The Story of a Bulgarian Boy in the Great American Melting Pot*, an autobiographical novel by Peter Yankoff, a Bulgarian-American author, as

> a two-room hut with walls of sundried bricks made from mud and straw. The inner walls were plastered and whitewashed to the roof. There was no ceiling. For a roof, homemade tiles rested on rafters supported by arched beams. The floor was of dirt, coated with clay which had been mixed with manure. The house was divided into two rooms by a low partition over which a grown person could look. In the winter, the family occupied

one room, and the livestock the other. The window opening to the outside world was about two feet by three feet. Over this a curtain was hung. Light reached the room by this window, the door as it might be opened, and the wide chimney of the fireplace.

By the 20th century, the Bulgarian peasantry had a long tradition of emigration in search of economic opportunity. For centuries the Bulgars had traveled abroad as migrant workers, the *burchevii*. These seasonal laborers went to Hungary, Russia, and Romania in search of farm work and a good wage. The burchevii often stayed away for years, working in teams or gangs, saving all the money they could for their return home. The first Bulgarian immigrants to America reenacted this tradition; most of the men who left economically troubled Bulgaria expected to return after they had made a modest fortune.

In this photograph from 1935, a Bulgarian peasant uses a wooden plow of the sort used by farmers in his country for 2,000 years. In the early decades of the 20th century, Bulgaria was a country of tiny parcels of land individually owned by peasants and farmed by primitive means.

Another sector of Bulgarian society also had experience in leaving their homeland, at least temporarily, to take advantage of opportunities abroad. In the 1880s, American Protestant missionaries began sending teachers to Bulgaria. These educators in turn sent gifted Bulgarian pupils to America or Western Europe to further their studies. For many young Bulgarians, the Protestant church helped realize a dream of higher education that could not be reached in their own country. Some stayed in the United States, while others returned to Bulgaria, where they were instrumental in introducing new educational, scientific, and agricultural theories. Although the American missionaries succeeded in converting only 26,000 members of the Bulgarian Orthodox church, their influence was much greater in terms of bringing news of the modern world to an isolated people.

The most persuasive reason for Bulgarians to make the long trip to America was its famed prosperity. Steamship agents traveled throughout Eastern Europe recruiting laborers for American industry and passengers for their ships by telling stories of the wonders to be found in the New World. In an interview conducted with Bulgarians in Chicago, Illinois, in 1908, 77 percent said that their emigration had been influenced by the visit of a steamship agent to their village, 12 percent said that family or friends had convinced them to come to America, and 11 percent said that they had come on their own initiative.

Stoyan Christowe, Vermont state senator and novelist, emigrated to America from Bulgaria as a teenager in 1912. In his book entitled *This Is My Country*, Christowe describes how the words of the steamship agents fired the imagination of his people, inspiring an obsession he called "Americamania": "Americamania . . . changed the life of the village. People mortgaged fields and vineyards and meadows to the merchants in the towns for enough money for the passage to this new world." Letters arriving from America supported the agents' claims; more than one immigrant wrote home to say that he was earning more in one day than he could earn in a week at home. When money orders began arriving from family members in America, even skeptics had to acknowledge that America could be a land of opportunity. The image of America as a land of plenty was further fostered by returning burchevii. "The emigrants, dazzled by America," wrote Christowe, "told of what they saw, of the money they earned, the work they were doing, but not of what was happening to themselves." They returned with money, new clothes, and an attitude of sophistication. They awed the villagers with stories of a country that considered electricity, elevators, and skyscrapers everyday phenomena.

The Journey

Those willing to leave behind all that was familiar faced serious initial difficulties. Financing the $100 (equivalent to $5,000 today) journey with the meager resources available to the average peasant could be an insurmountable obstacle. The only collateral a peasant had

Many Macedonian Bulgarians left for North America on ships that departed from Greek ports. Before boarding, they were processed through emigration stations like this one in Patras, Greece.

to offer was his animals and his farm. Because there were no banks in rural Bulgaria at the turn of the century, peasants turned to local moneylenders or merchants and hoped they could strike a fair deal. All too often interest rates charged on mortgages were in excess of 20 percent a year. Such high rates would ruin a man denied entry to the United States. Some men committed suicide on being turned away at U.S. ports; to return to Bulgaria meant to return to nothing.

Bulgaria's ports were small and handled little transoceanic transport; finding a ship to America meant traveling to another European port. Macedonians usually bought passage on a Greek ship sailing from the ports of Piraeus or Salonika, while Bulgarians were more likely to take a boat up the Danube River to Vienna, where they boarded a train to ports in France, Germany, or Italy, such as Le Havre, Brest, Hamburg, Bremen, Trieste, or Genoa.

In *Peter Menikoff: The Story of a Bulgarian Boy in the Great American Melting Pot*, Peter Yankoff described a Bulgarian emigrant's journey to America. On his way to the ships in Hamburg, Germany, Yankoff's train was stopped in Leipzig so that the authorities could check the health and passports of the emigrants. He wrote: "It seemed that Leipzig was the converging point of every railway in the world and every emigrant train . . . made that city their final destination." The crowds of emigrants were so huge and poorly organized that "husbands were separated from their wives, children from their parents and friends from their friends." Surprisingly, "the examination of each person and certification of each passport" was done quickly and efficiently because "there was a whole array of doctors, nurses, and state officials." At the completion of an examination the emigrant "was let out through a backdoor, which made the reunion of friends and families a very difficult problem, especially for those who were ignorant of the German language."

When they arrived in a port city, the emigrants were processed by their host country and kept in a detention

camp reserved for transients until the ships docked. When Yankoff arrived in Hamburg, he was loaded onto a "train of flat cars pulled by street motors." Germans lined the streets to stare at the colorful variety of peasant emigrants, and reporters snapped photos of them for the newspapers; "the curious crowds followed the emigrant train to the very gates of the detention camp which was located on the outskirts of the city."

The camps were filthy places, and many of the government officials were corrupt. The few available beds were infected with lice. A meal consisted of "four stale rolls and a tin cup of tasteless coffee." The service was so slow and the emigrants so hungry that "everybody ran like a bunch of starved swine . . . and the people grew so excited and unruly that the officers in charge were compelled to call for help." Yankoff

Slavic immigrants pose at the U.S. immigration station at Ellis Island. Early immigration statistics on Bulgarian and Macedonian-Bulgarian immigrants are confusing. Until 1920, Bulgarians from "the kingdom" were grouped with Serbians and Montenegrins; ethnic Bulgarians were classified as Russian, Romanian, Serbian, or Greek depending on their last place of residence and the current national borders.

reflected that "life in a detention camp for emigrants proved to be much worse than even that of prison life."

Ironically, the emigrants' health was carefully monitored: "Every morning at ten o'clock, the emigrants stood in line to be examined by a corps of physicians. They closely examined eyes, nose, ears, and teeth; but strange to relate, they were at the same time utterly indifferent to the conditions of the emigrant lodgings."

There was little to do to pass the time while in detention except wait and perhaps long for home. After more than a week's time, camp officials called the weary

Bulgarian immigrants George Zekoff (later Grekoff) and Sofia Amirov Nenew. The two were both widowed with children when they married; they left Bulgaria in 1918 and spent time in Romania, Greece, and France. Ultimately, George left the family in order to establish a place for them in the United States, and the family was finally reunited when George was granted a homestead in Steele, North Dakota.

emigrants one by one to board the ships for a voyage that could last as long as a month. Most of the poor occupied steerage, or third class, in the hold of the ship. Profit, not sanitation, was the captain's priority; the result for the steerage passengers was thick, unventilated air, soiled, cramped living space, foul water, and poor food. Passengers suffered from seasickness as well as from contagious diseases, such as the common cold, influenza, and diarrhea, which spread rapidly under the unsanitary conditions. To escape the fetid squalor below, steerage passengers spent as much time as possible above deck; unfortunately, the rolling of the ship often only worsened their misery.

In spite of the often demeaning hardships, most immigrants arrived in the New World worn down but not seriously ill. Those who suspected that they would be denied legal entry into the United States planned methods of illegal entrance. The most daring might jump ship in sight of New York City and swim ashore. The majority chose to come through Mexico or Canada to avoid the more stringent U.S. immigration authorities.

After passing a battery of medical tests as part of processing at the immigration station at Ellis Island, the immigrant faced the daunting task of finding a home and a job. Most followed the advice of family or friends who had immigrated before them. Because the work most easily obtained by uneducated and unskilled laborers was to be found in railroad construction, factory work, and mining, most Bulgarian immigrants spent the last of their funds traveling to the industrial cities of Pittsburgh, Detroit, Chicago, and Granite City and the nearby regions.

The majority of the Bulgarians who came to America in the early years of the 20th century were either bachelors or married men traveling without their families, and neither group expected to settle in the United States or Canada permanently. Their goal was to earn enough money to enable them to return to

The Zekoff family's passport listed those members traveling with the head of the family. Their original name, Zekoff, was recorded incorrectly by immigration officials at Ellis Island; thereafter, most members of the family referred to themselves as Grekoff. George, the father, died in 1946; Sofia, the mother, died in 1982 at the age of 91.

Bulgaria and purchase a farm of their own. Nevertheless, a number of Bulgarian immigrants did intend to establish a more permanent way of life in America. Those who planned on staying often hoped to make their living from the land, as they had done in Bulgaria.

Between 1910 and 1914, a small group of perhaps 20 Bulgarian families came to America via the southeastern European region of Bessarabia, then under the control of Russia. According to William C. Sherman in *Prairie Mosaic: An Ethnic Atlas of Rural North Dakota*, these families had emigrated to Bessarabia in the middle of the 19th century and were living in dire poverty when the report of a German-Russian villager who had settled in North Dakota encouraged them to try homesteading in the American Midwest. But by the time the Bulgarians arrived in Kidder, Logan, and Stutsman counties, North Dakota, the homesteads had all been claimed, and most of the immigrants were forced instead to rent small holdings and work for local farmers. Some found work on the railroads. In 1917, several families moved to homesteads in Custer and Powder River counties in Montana, but by 1920, the isolation and shortage of good land had brought many of the settlers back to North Dakota. Perhaps because of the training in hardship they had received during their first years in America, these Bulgarian Americans managed to maintain a strong sense of community for at least three decades. Today, largely because of intermarriage, the third and fourth generation's minimal exposure to traditional customs, and its dispersal throughout the state, the North Dakota Bulgarian-American community is less insular and a good deal more assimilated. It has also achieved a significant measure of economic success. Many of its members own substantial land holdings and specialize in raising purebred cattle.

According to Nikolay G. Altankov, author of *The Bulgarian-Americans*, in the early years of the 20th century a number of Bulgarians settled in and around Minneapolis-St. Paul, where they grew produce for

market; another sizable Bulgarian immigrant community made its home in Yakima, Washington, where many of them earned their living as fruit growers. Many of their descendants still reside in the Yakima area. By 1918, Bulgarians had also established farming communities in Tulsa, Oklahoma, and Kent, Ohio, but these rural communities remained the exception. Most Bulgarians in America were more likely to spend their long work days in a grimy mill, mine, or factory than in a sunlit field.

The Wesalenko family, close friends of the Grekoff family, pose with an automobile in North Dakota.

Lewis W. Hine, whose work documents the life of immigrants in America in the early 20th century, photographed these Pennsylvania coal miners in 1910. Generally uneducated and unskilled, Bulgarian immigrants were forced to lead a nomadic life, seeking job opportunities as they became available—in coal mines, on railroads, or in steel mills.

THE FIRST GENERATION

The Bulgarian immigrant of the early 20th century was confronted with a reality that bore little resemblance to his dreams. Finding work was often harder than the immigrant had imagined it would be, for jobs were often controlled by unscrupulous labor agents. For example, a man might be given five days' work at a wage of one dollar a day; the employment agency might then charge him seven dollars for the placement. By 1900, members of the older immigrant groups, such as the Irish, were moving on to higher-paying skilled work, leaving the least desirable jobs open for newcomers. Physical labor in mills, factories, slaughterhouses, and on railway gangs required few language skills and no previous experience. Nevertheless, during the depression of 1907 and other times of widespread unemployment in America, Bulgarian immigrants were resented for taking work from more well established Americans. Members of labor unions feared that the willingness of Bulgarian and other eastern and southern European immigrants to work for low wages would undercut the hard-won gains of the labor movement, and they also feared that the Bulgarians would be used as strikebreakers.

Railroad work was popular with Bulgarian immigrants because it generally required workers to spend long periods away from home, which in many cases were squalid apartments or crowded boardinghouses in urban areas that were little more than ghettos; employers paid for lodging and food during the working season, which enabled workers to save a good part of their earnings. Dangerous jobs such as dynamite blasting for the railroad or operating potentially deadly machinery in the steel industry attracted the immigrant worker because of the better pay they offered, but they required a costly trade-off: Work-related accidents were the greatest cause of death among young immigrant men.

Most laborers worked 12-hour shifts, 6 or 7 days a week. Long hours meant more money to take home.

Workers operate a trip-hammer in a steel mill in Pittsburgh, Pennsylvania in the early 1900s. Pittsburgh is home to one of America's oldest Bulgarian communities. Immigrants from eastern Europe were drawn to Pittsburgh and other Pennsylvania cities such as Steelton because of the availability of work in steel mills and foundries.

Although a railroad worker could expect to earn only between $1.50 and $6.25 per day, prices for staples were low, and a particularly thrifty worker might save as much as $50 each month. According to reports of the Federal Immigration Commission, the average yearly earnings of an immigrant laborer between 1903 and 1908 were $455.

Between 1903 and 1908, the peak years of Bulgarian and Macedonian immigration, there arose a need for community assistance, mutual aid, and cultural organizations to help the new residents adjust to life in America. Eventually, the Bulgarian Americans established three different types of societies: mutual benefit organizations, many of which had a religious affiliation; nationalist groups devoted to the ideal of an independent Macedonia or unification with Bulgaria; and political associations interested in broad issues, the most important of which were leftist organizations (in the years before the conclusion of World War II) and the more recent anti-Communist fronts.

The Protestant denominations, which had long maintained a missionary presence in the Balkans, were the first American religious organizations to rally to the aid of the Bulgarian immigrants. In fact, Bulgarians who had been educated at the American school in Samokov, Bulgaria, or at Robert College in Constantinople were already serving as ministers in America. Protestant ministers sought out Bulgarian immigrants in their ethnic enclaves; in 1907, Pastor Bagranoff and his wife established in Madison, Illinois, the first mission specifically devoted to the aim of providing religious instruction, general education, and elementary social skills to the Bulgarian newcomers. The mission gave English lessons in an evening school for adults and offered courses in American history, civics, and geography. A small library provided literature in Bulgarian and English. More than 1,300 immigrants attended Pastor Bagranoff's school during its first 10 years of existence. During the winter months, the pastor and his wife helped the immigrants maintain traditional village customs by staging native plays and other cultural events.

The most serious problem the immigrant faced was unemployment. In 1908, at least 4,000 Bulgarian immigrants were without work. The Bagranoffs publicized the Bulgarians' plight and raised money to support many immigrants until they found jobs. In all, the Bagranoffs helped find employment for 1,500 immigrants; their mission and others like it—notably in St. Louis, Missouri; Kansas City, Kansas; and Toledo, Ohio—were more dedicated to helping the immigrant than to converting him or her. In 1937, there were five Protestant missions for Bulgarians in the United States and three in Canada. The missions continued to thrive until a decreasing number of immigrants and the long-term economic pressures of the Great Depression forced them to close down.

Benefit societies were also organized by the immigrants themselves. For example, in 1906, Iliia Iovchev, an employee at the Immigration Bureau at Ellis Island, founded the Bulgarian and Macedonian Immigrant Society Prishelets (Newcomer), the first Bulgarian-American mutual benefit and cultural society. Between 1907 and 1913, almost 30 mutual benefit and educational societies were formed. By 1933, 200 such groups claimed a total membership of 10,000. A typical example is the Babchorsko Beneficial Society VICH, founded in Fort Wayne, Indiana, on October 7, 1912; by 1918, the society boasted 120 members, all former residents of the village of Babchor in Greek Macedonia. Members vowed to assist each other both morally and materially and to give financial support to their native town.

The first Bulgarian women's charitable and educational organization, Bulgarkata v Amerika (Bulgarian Women in America), was founded on September 25, 1913. Meetings were devoted to such diverse topics as child rearing and American politics. The organization assisted poor and sick Bulgarian Americans and during

the First World War collected money for the Bulgarian Red Cross.

As Bulgarian communities grew, their inhabitants naturally desired their own houses of worship. On June 9, 1908, two Bulgarian priests sent by the Holy Synod in Sofia arrived in Granite City, Illinois. On September 14, 1909, the first Bulgarian Orthodox church in America, St. Cyril and St. Methody, was dedicated there. Not long afterward, the second, Holy Annunciation, opened its doors in Steelton, Pennsylvania. Over the next few decades the Bulgarian church in America flourished; until 1938, all recognized the ultimate jurisdiction of the Holy Synod in Sofia. In January of 1938, the Holy Synod created the Bishopric for the Americas; the titular bishop remained responsible to Sofia, and his authority went largely unrecognized in North America. However, once a Communist government took control in the homeland, Bulgarian Americans began to question whether a church answerable to a government ideologically opposed to religion could long maintain its

A group portrait of the Elenora Club taken in Gary, Indiana, in 1927. The club's members were the wives of Bulgarians and Macedonian Bulgarians. Most women's organizations concerned themselves with charity work that benefited both the local community and their native villages and stressed patriotic allegiance to both the United States and Bulgaria.

ЕКОНОМИЧЕСКОТО
ОБЯСНЕНИЕ на РАБОТАТА

BULGARIAN—AN ECONOMIC INTERPRETATION OF THE JOB

Цѣна 25 цента

Издание на
ИНДУСТРИАЛНИТѢ РАБОТНИЦИ НА СВѢТА
1001 W. MADISON ST., CHICAGO, ILL.

This 1923 pamphlet, written in Bulgarian, was published by an American labor organization and addressed to the common worker. Bulgarian Americans had long demonstrated a keen interest in labor issues. On April 7, 1908, a group of unemployed Bulgarians marched on Chicago's City Hall demanding work. The protest publicized their plight, and several charitable organizations offered temporary relief.

freedom and meet the needs of its faithful. In 1948, Andrei Velichki, a bishop of the Bulgarian church in America, refused to recognize the authority of the Holy Synod, a decision that touched off almost 20 years of angry and complicated administrative struggles. By 1963, there were two separate administrations of the Bulgarian church outside of Bulgaria. The loyalist faction called itself the Bulgarian Eastern Orthodox Church Diocese of North and South America and Australia and acknowledged the supreme authority of the Holy Synod in Sofia, while the Diocese of the United States and Canada of the Bulgarian Eastern Orthodox Church, which claimed the allegiance of nine churches, denied Sofia's ultimate jurisdiction. Today, the Bulgarian-American community continues to be divided in its loyalties but remains united in its belief.

Overtly political organizations played an important role in the lives of the first generation of Bulgarians and Macedonians in America. For example, after the Bulgarian defeat in the Balkan Wars, Ieromanach Teofilakt and others held the first meeting of the All-Bulgarian Congress in Chicago. Its objective was to unify the Bulgarians in America and Canada and to work toward the goal of Macedonian autonomy. Chapters were founded in all of the major Bulgarian communities in the midwestern United States and in Toronto, Canada. At the height of its influence, the congress published a daily newspaper called *Syoboda* (Liberty).

A small number of Bulgarians and Macedonians actively participated in the American Socialist movement. The Bulgarian Socialist Labor Federation was founded in 1910 by the unification of a handful of splinter groups; seven years later it joined the larger and more influential American Socialist Labor Party (SLP). For the next 30 years, a large number of tiny Socialist and Communist groups were founded, merged, and dissolved. Some followed such American Socialist leaders as Daniel De Leon, while others fell in behind the American branch of IMRO, led by V. I. Poptomov.

Throughout the 1920s and 1930s, Bulgarian political activists joined the Communist Party of the United States of America (CPUSA) in support of striking industrial and mine workers, and many participated in antifascist congresses.

In 1922, Macedonian Bulgarians in America formed the Union of Macedonian Political Organizations (MPO) which, according to Nikolay Altankov, is "still the most vital and energetic clearinghouse of Macedonian Bulgarian ideas and activities in the continent of North America." The MPO's central aim is to "work and struggle legally towards the establishment of Macedonia as an independent republic within its geographical and economic boundaries, which is to guarantee to the fullest the democratic, social, and economic rights and liberties, duties, and privileges of all its citizens." Since 1926, the MPO has published the *Makedonska Tribuna* (Macedonian Tribune), which today is the only Bulgarian-language weekly in America. In

Members enjoy dinner at the 16th Annual Convention of the Macedonian Political (later Patriotic) Organization (MPO), held in Indianapolis, Indiana, in September 1937. Founded in 1922, the MPO believes that all Macedonians are ethnic Bulgarians and supports the idea of a united and independent Macedonia.

МАКЕДОНСКА ТРИБУНА

Makedonska Tribuna ~ Macedonian Tribune

Give me Liberty, or Give me Death! — Patrick Henry   Address: MACEDONIAN TRIBUNE—107 S. Capitol Ave., Indianapolis, Indiana 46225 U.S.A.   Telephone: 635-3587

29 ЯНУАРИЙ 1970 ГОД., ГОД. 43, БР. 2,219   Second Class Postage paid at Indianapolis, Indiana   VOLUME 43, NUMBER 2,219   JANUARY 29, 1970

Относно книгата на Д. Казасовъ "Видѣно и преживѣно"

Великата лъжа
ИЛИ
«ИСТОРИЯ НА МАКЕДОНСКИОТ НАРОД»

ПОСЛАНИЕТО НА ПРЕЗИДЕНТА

A GREEK SCHOLAR REBUKES THE "ACADEMICIANS" OF SKOPIE

BY CHRISTO N. NIZAMOFF

Балкански новини

Since 1927 the MPO has published the weekly newspaper Makedonska Tribuna. *On the front page of the January 29, 1970, edition can be seen, in English, the words of American patriot Patrick Henry: "Give me Liberty, or give me Death!"*

1952, the MPO changed its name to the Macedonian Patriotic Organization.

In 1944, a nonsectarian, anti-Communist organization was formed in Chicago, Illinois. The American Bulgarian League boasted a largely educated and professional membership; its goals included the nurturing of Bulgarian cultural values as well as the promotion of a greater understanding between the United States and Bulgaria. In 1956, the league became a member of the Conference of Americans of Central Eastern European Descent, a group intent on coordinating the efforts of all Americans from Central and Eastern Europe devoted to the liberation of their homelands from Communist regimes. The American Bulgarian League also helped many displaced Bulgarians make their way to America.

Life in the City

No matter how much support an immigrant received from his fellow compatriots, daily life for most Bulgarian Americans was generally a struggle. The "little

Bulgarias" in Chicago, New York, and Detroit and the "Hungary Hollow" of Granite City, Illinois, a quarter that supported 15,000 residents at its peak, were some of the least sanitary and most overcrowded areas in their respective cities. Immigrants who worked long, exhausting hours had little time or energy to improve their surroundings; often, city governments were also slow to provide services to areas where the majority of the citizens were not citizens and thus unable to vote. An official 1913 report on Granite City noted that "sanitary supervision was conspicuous by its absence." Streets were unpaved, and outdoor latrines were not uncommon. The presence of vermin and the problem of overcrowded apartments further threatened the public health.

According to the reports of the Federal Immigration Commission, the majority of Bulgarian immigrants lived in groups and shared household management and

As seen in this 1895 photograph, Bohemian Flats, a section of Minneapolis, Minnesota, was a typical midwestern Slavic settlement, similar to the ones Bulgarians would establish by the 1920s.

expenses. In his early writings, Stoyan Christowe describes the St. Louis house where he first lived in the United States:

> There were six men in the flat at the moment and they worked days, sharing the six beds with a like number of men who worked nights. In other words, there were twelve men living in the two-room flat. The beds, placed lengthwise along the walls in the room overlooking the street, were never given a rest or an airing. There were no sheets and the blankets and the comfortables were so filthy with coal dust and grease they looked like tarpaulins.

A Bulgarian immigrant who had been in America long enough to have purchased a house and to have sent for his wife might operate a *boort*, or boardinghouse. The landlord, or "boarding boss," rented out as much of the house as he could, often to the detriment of his own health and that of his family. The boarding boss worked a regular job in a mine or a factory; his wife was burdened with the enormous job of raising her children and providing dinner and laundry services for as many as 20 boarders, most of them single men from the same village in Bulgaria who were now working at the same factory. Conditions in the boorts were frequently as bad as those the immigrants had endured in steerage, and overcrowding contributed to a high infant mortality rate for children born to the boarding boss's wife and to the rapid spread of contagious diseases among all inhabitants. Boarding bosses were less concerned with comfortable living conditions than they were with making a profit large enough to enable them to buy a business or to return home as wealthy men.

The squalor of immigrant ghettos may be attributed to several factors. As a recently arrived and numerically small group, Bulgarian immigrants faced discrimination in both housing and employment opportunities;

(continued on page 73)

COMMUNION AND COMMUNITY

By encouraging children to participate in religious ceremonies
and the social life of the church (overleaf, right, and above), the
Bulgarian-American community reaffirms the importance of
family life, passes its traditions on to the younger generation,
and ensures that the Bulgarian Orthodox church in America
will continue to thrive.

The children of St. Cyril and St. Methody parish in Granite City, Illinois, put on a Christmas pageant in December 1989. The first Bulgarian Orthodox church in America was founded in 1909; more than 80 years later the Bulgarian Orthodox church continues to serve as the center of the community's spiritual and ethnic life.

In 1989, Alex Tarpoff, president of St. Cyril and St. Methody in Granite City, Illinois, joined church leaders, including the American Metropolitan (above), in celebrating the consecration and laying of the cornerstone of the new church building. Behind the scenes (right), parishioners prepared a feast of traditional foods. The Bulgarian Orthodox faith is traditionally the most crucial element of a strong sense of national pride that flourishes even in America.

Bulgarian Americans express pride in their heritage in secular as well as in spiritual rites. In 1980, members of the Bosilek Bulgarian Dance Troupe participated in the annual One World Festival in New York City (above). Bulgarian folk music and dance has experienced a surge of popularity in both the Bulgarian-American and the larger community in recent years.

The preponderance of unmarried males among most eastern and southern European immigrant groups led to the proliferation of boardinghouse arrangements, in which a large group of immigrant men, such as the ones seen here, would share living quarters. The boardinghouses in which Bulgarians lived were known as boorts.

(continued from page 64)

when employers and city officials ignored the Bulgarians' basic needs, there was little an immigrant could do to significantly better his working and living conditions, particularly when the ballot box was not available as a last resort. Indeed, in some ways the Bulgarian community was invisible to the larger urban population; for example, Bulgarian children were largely absent from the public school system because most were still in Bulgaria with their mothers. When Bulgarian children were first sent to school in America, they often attended schools affiliated with the Orthodox church. Although this helped maintain traditional ways and values, it contributed to the relative isolation of the Bulgarians within the larger community. But, according to Altankov, a good deal of the community's isolation and of the overcrowding in urban areas was a matter of choice on the part of the immigrants, who saw themselves as temporary residents and were primarily concerned with earning as much as they could as quickly as possible.

A group of men relax at a café in Kutlowitza, Bulgaria, in the early 1900s. Bulgarians in America established the kafene, *a version of the traditional café, as a place where they could eat, drink, and talk Bulgarian politics. Along with the boort, the kafene was an integral feature of the Bulgarian-American community.*

In spite of backbreaking work and poor living conditions, the Bulgarian immigrant worker did enjoy some pleasures. After a long day of work he could go to a *kafene*, or coffeehouse, where he might enjoy the companionship of his countrymen while partaking of coffee, tea, cider, lemonade, tobacco, or traditional foods. (A more prosperous kafene could afford refrigeration and might offer ice cream and soda as well.) Men played cards or backgammon while discussing the most recent political developments in the homeland. Because most kafene owners had been in America for some time, they were generally acknowledged to be the most intelligent men of the Bulgarian community. The kafene owner often acted as everything from interpreter to attorney for his clients; his kafene functioned as an information center, newsstand,

and vendor of stamps, international money orders, and steamship tickets.

Permanent Communities

With little variation, this picture of Bulgarian-American urban life was repeated in almost all factory and mill towns where Bulgarian immigrants settled, but in the 1920s the nature of Bulgarian immigrant communities began to change. Once men sent for wives and families, permanent communities began to be established. In 1908, there were an estimated 20 Bulgarian settlements in America; by 1930, that number had risen to 700. By the early 1930s, Los Angeles, California; Chicago, Granite City, and Madison, Illinois; Indianapolis, Fort Wayne, and Gary, Indiana; Detroit, Michigan; St. Louis, Missouri; New York, Rochester, and Lackawanna, New York; Cleveland, Youngstown, Akron, Massilon, and Columbus, Ohio; and Steelton, Pennsylvania, each maintained Bulgarian settlements of over 500 inhabitants. In 1933, over 7,000 people of Bulgarian descent made their home in Detroit, which made that city home to the largest single settlement of Bulgarian Americans.

While most Bulgarians lived in or around cities, a minority settled in more isolated areas. Besides the communities in Washington State and North Dakota mentioned previously, Bulgarians wishing to live closer to the land settled in such places as Sofia, New Mexico, and in Oklahoma and Ohio. Those Bulgarian-American urban dwellers who chose to remain in America invested their savings in bakeries, luncheonettes, dry goods stores, boorts, kafenes, and saloons. The more ambitious might establish a "bank" of sorts, which, according to Nikolay Altankov was "a bureau for information and a clearinghouse of services" for a specific immigrant population. The banks received money for safekeeping, arranged for money to be sent overseas, and purchased steamship tickets for families

Although the majority of Bulgarian immigrants in North America chose urban rather than rural life, some did seek out homesteads in places like North Dakota and in various parts of Canada. This picture, taken in the 1920s, shows Mr. Floro, a Bulgarian immigrant, sitting atop a tractor on a farm at Port Hope, Ontario.

still in Bulgaria. They also served as centers of information for the Bulgarian-American community and offered books and magazines to interested readers. The owner of such a bank was often a political leader of sorts and often also owned a boort, bakery, employment agency, or saloon.

For those Bulgarians who chose to forge a life in America, family relations, at least through the first generation, followed traditional Bulgarian patterns of a close-knit patriarchy. The father made all important decisions; the mother was his helpmate. Grandparents played a large role in raising children, who were treated with both discipline and respect, and all social life centered around the extended family. However, certain aspects of life in America at the beginning of the century contributed to the breakdown of traditional family structure. Perhaps the most influential was the "atomization tendency" of American society at the time, which coincided with the rapid growth of industrialization and urbanization. The result was a change in the structure of the American family to allow for a more equitable balance of power within the home and an increasing acceptance of each family member's individual goals. With more and more people working outside of the home, the American family, and, by extension, the immigrant family, was gradually becoming more mobile and its members more independent. As the children of first-generation Bulgarian immigrants attended school and acquired a command of the English language, as well as an increased understanding and awareness of American society, a sort of generation gap was formed. As took place within so many immigrant groups, the second generation was eager to assimilate in order to achieve greater economic success than their parents, even if the process of assimilation required abandoning certain basic elements of the Bulgarian heritage.

Several children and their father listen closely to the plaintive sound of a traditional pigskin bagpipe near the town of Plovdiv in Bulgaria in 1935.

A RICH CULTURAL HERITAGE

Although the Bulgarian Americans are a small ethnic population, their contribution to the fields of music, literature, and art is significant. Bulgarian folk dancing is enjoying a popularity among both Bulgarian and non-Bulgarian groups in America. Traditional Bulgarian music has been a source of inspiration for many Western musicians, such as the Americans Paul Simon and David Byrne, the English singer Kate Bush, and the Scottish group Simple Minds. Translations of Bulgarian classics as well as other memoirs, fiction, poetry, and nonfiction written by Bulgarian-American authors are easily found in public libraries, and Bulgarian cuisine is appreciated by those who enjoy hearty and flavorful food.

Music and Dance

Perhaps the richest aspect of the Bulgarian cultural heritage is its traditional music and song. Through 500 years of Turkish domination, the Bulgarian people held fast to their music as a vehicle of both community and personal expression. Even today, music is an integral part of daily life; the Bulgarian people continue to sing traditional songs commemorating births, marriages, deaths, religious holidays, harvests, and festivals.

Traditional Bulgarian music, with its irregular beat, unusual harmonies, and nasal style of singing, often sounds strange to Western ears. Although it is lively and suitable for dancing, Bulgarian music employs an irregular beat. Recently, the Trio Bulgarka, female singers in the traditional style, appeared in New York City with other members of the Bulgarian State Ensemble for Folk Music and Dance. At one point in the performance, two women in brightly embroidered native dress sang in the traditional style without musical accompaniment, one voice weaving flourishes around the drone of the other. At another juncture, the women were joined by men playing traditional Bulgarian instruments, including a *ghaida*, a sort of goatskin bagpipe with a reed mouthpiece. Occasionally, the animal's fur and head adorn the instrument. Another man played a large, two-sided drum called a *tupan*. One man played an end-blown flute known as the *kaval*; another played the *zurna*, an oboelike wind instrument. The final two members of the band played the *gadulka* and *tamboura*, both stringed instruments.

Bulgarian dance, music, and song can be enjoyed in concert halls, churches, and ethnic folk art centers

The Selyani Macedonian Folklore Group posed in full costume for this photograph taken in Kingston, Ontario, in July 1976. At the time, the group was readying itself for a performance at the summer Olympic games in Montreal.

throughout North America. In recent years, an unprecendented interest in Bulgarian music has led increasing numbers of non-Bulgarians to take music and dance lessons. Carol Freeman, an American with no Bulgarian ancestry, became interested in Bulgarian singing as a result of her enjoyment of ethnic folk dancing. Freeman made several trips to Bulgaria to learn from the women who have been singing in the traditional way since childhood. Eventually, Freeman formed a three-person group called Zhenska Pesen, which means "women's songs." As a result of extensive research in Bulgaria, Freeman has a repertoire of over 1,000 songs. Since she founded Zhenska Pesen, there has been a growing interest in this unique style of singing, and large groups of people now participate in Bulgarian

Although maintenance of the Bulgarian language has declined in America, there has been a renewed interest in Bulgarian folk music and dance. The members of the popular group Balkana, *pictured here, performed traditional music at a successful benefit reception and dance party held at New York's Ethnic Folk Arts Center in April 1989.*

Two dancers adorned with cowbells, masks, and tall hats topped with dolls parade through the village of Turia, Bulgaria, as participants in the traditional kukeri carnival. This colorful festival draws people from all over Bulgaria as well as from abroad.

song workshops in California and West Virginia. Today, Freeman leads workshops and teaches privately in New York City.

Several collections of Bulgarian music are now available. The best known of these is the Bulgarian State Radio and Television Female Vocal Choir's *Le Mystère des Voix Bulgares*, released on the Elektra/Nonesuch label as part of its Explorer series. The record has sold more than 100,000 copies worldwide. Hannibal Records is competing with titles such as *Balkana: The Music of Bulgaria* and *The Forest Is Crying*, featuring Trio Bulgarka. *Le Chant des Femmes Bulgares*, from Harmonia Mundi, is also popular.

Trio Bulgarka has sung backup harmonies on several records for such recording artists as Kate Bush, and other popular Western musicians have created their own arrangements of Bulgarian songs. David Byrne's 1985 *Music for the Knee Plays* includes a brass-band version of "Theodora Is Dozing," entitled "Polegnala e Todora" on the *Mystère* album mentioned above. An England-based band known as 3 Mustaphas 3 sports fezzes, affects a broken English for their between-song banter, and plays Balkan music on both traditional and modern instruments, blending goatskin bagpipes with Western synthesizers. The band's keyboardist, who calls himself Kemo Mustapha, says that "what we're doing is bringing music that is very popular in the countries of origin to Western audiences; we like it, and we don't see why it shouldn't be heard."

Bulgarian folk songs speak of things heroic, religious, and historical. There are songs about farming and songs about love, marriage, and difficult mothers-in-law. There are songs about mourning and happiness and songs about local superstitions and mythical creatures. Some songs recount actual historical battles and their heroes. The lyrics of the following song lament the abuses suffered by the *raya*, the non-Muslim population, under Turkish rule.

Now are the furrows ready for sowing
Yet it is not seed that is sown in them.
For they are bestrewn with bullets and corpses
And they are besprinkled with hero's blood.
Upon the field there lies the young hero,
Out of his breast the dark blood is flowing
He lies in the field that is ready for sowing,
With no one to bury him or bewail him;
No mother has he to shed tears over him,
No father has he to put earth over him,
Only the ravens—they float over him.

Unfortunately, many traditional customs and songs have disappeared as Bulgaria's population has made the transition from a rural, isolated, and agricultural way of life to an urban, industrial, and centralized one. Today, the most likely place to hear Bulgarian folk music in its traditional setting is in the isolated mountain villages and in some Muslim communities.

Several Bulgarians have established international careers as opera singers. The bass Nicolai Ghiaurov was

Born in 1929 in Velingrad, Bulgaria, bass singer Nicolai Ghiaurov made his 1955 debut in Sofia as Don Basilio in Rossini's Il Barbiere di Siviglia. Ghiaurov is only one of several Bulgarians, including the New York–based singer-turned-talent-agent Lyubomir Vichey, who have achieved success in the classical music world.

83

born in Velingrad, Bulgaria, on September 13, 1929. He studied first at the Sofia Conservatory and then at the Moscow Conservatory. In 1963, Ghiaurov made his U.S. debut in Chicago; in 1965, he made his debut at New York City's Metropolitan Opera in Charles Gounod's *Faust*. Critics agree that Ghiaurov's powerful voice and Slavic background have made him particularly impressive in the great roles in Russian opera. The talented soprano Ljuba Welitsch was born in Borisovo, Bulgaria, on July 10, 1913; she became a regular member of the Vienna State Opera in 1946. Welitsch made her U.S. debut in 1949 at the Metropolitan Opera in her signature role as Salome, the heroine of Richard Strauss's opera of the same name. She is best remembered for her silvery soprano and her passionate onstage personality. The sopranos Ghena Dimitrova, Anna Tomowa-Sintow, and Raina Kabaivanska are among the many Bulgarians who have established successful careers in the classical music world.

Literature

In the mid-19th century, the Bulgarian language, long suppressed by the Turks, began to reassert itself. In 1835, the first Bulgarian school was founded, and in 1838, the first Bulgarian printing press began operating in Salonika. The first Bulgarian-language newspaper rolled off the presses in 1846. All these developments led to the flowering of Bulgarian literature that took place in the 1860s.

Twenty-six-year-old Ivan Vazov was one of the organizers of the 1876 April Uprising for his hometown of Sopot, in the the Tundzha River valley. When the rebellion failed, Vazov fled to Romania. In 1878, after Bulgaria had won independence from the Ottoman Empire, Vazov returned to Sopot and discovered that the town had been destroyed and that his father had been killed by the bashi-bazooks. Moved by his experiences, Vazov set out to communicate them in writing. *Under the Yoke*, written between 1887 and 1889, is one of the first Bulgarian novels. It tells the harrowing story of the April 1876 uprising and describes both the spirit of revolution and the violence of the Turkish reprisals. Translated into English in 1971, the novel is generally considered a classic and helped Vazov earn his reputation as one of the fathers of Bulgarian literature.

Several Bulgarian Americans have written fascinating autobiographies. The best known is Stoyan Christowe's *Eagle and the Stork*, published by Harper's Magazine Press in 1976. Christowe tells of his decision to leave Macedonia and describes his struggles as a newcomer working on the railroads and then as a college student. In 1961, Christowe became a Vermont state senator. Since then he has written several volumes of memoirs as well as nonfiction concerning the political situation in Bulgaria.

Peter Dimitrov Yankoff, born in Bulgaria in 1885, published a slightly fictionalized account of his life in 1928, entitled *Peter Menikoff: The Story of a Bulgarian Boy in the Great American Melting Pot*. In 1940, Bulgarian immigrant Boris George Petroff told his story in *Son of the Danube*.

Food

According to Michael and Frances Field, authors of *A Quintet of Cuisines*, Bulgarian cooking, as well as that of most Balkan countries, has as its base the primary elements of Turkish cooking, a fact not surprising considering the 500 years Bulgaria spent *pod igoto*—under the yoke—of the Turks. Still, Bulgarian cooking can be distinguished from that of its neighbors; for example, Bulgarian dishes are usually spicier than their Romanian counterparts. And though it may not be as widely known as, for example, Greek food, it is no less exciting.

Although the contemporary tourist has little trouble finding appetizing traditional foods in a restaurant or in

A man sells traditional Bulgarian basket plates for a penny apiece in Detroit in 1943. Bulgarian folkcraft has changed little since the Middle Ages. After Bulgaria gained its independence in 1878, folkcraft flourished during a period known as the national revival. Today, Bulgarians and Bulgarian Americans attend folk festivals at which embroidered clothing, woven rugs, ceramics, and works made of gold, copper, and wood are sold.

a *mekhana* (tavern), Bulgaria has no restaurant tradition; families ate at home, and travelers stopped in monasteries for their meals. In modern times, the Bulgarian government has played an active part in the business of feeding its people. The government sets restaurant standards that emphasize cleanliness, nutrition, and economy rather than sophisticated cuisine. People with special dietary restrictions are provided with three meals a day at inexpensive, state-run restaurants; those who wish to eat with their families can take their meals home.

The Fields, who traveled to Bulgaria to research their book, assure their readers that contemporary Bulgaria offers visitors fresh and hearty fare. The Bulgarians place great emphasis on fresh vegetables, cheeses, nuts, and yogurt. *Sirene*, a brined goat cheese similar to Greek feta, is a Bulgarian specialty. Beautiful walnut groves grace the Tundzha River valley; the meat of the walnut is essential to a variety of dishes, including *tarator*, a cold cucumber, walnut, and yogurt soup sprinkled with dill. *Givetch*, a vegetable and meat stew, is spiced with hot green peppers and topped with a tempting crust of yogurt and beaten eggs. The Fields point out that as a result of the government's emphasis on the nutritional value of dairy products, meat is generally of an inferior quality. Most often it is used for dishes where its toughness is not as noticeable; *kebabche*, a sausage of veal and pork subtly seasoned with garlic, is a favorite. Breads are often elaborate; a "bird of paradise" loaf is decorated with triangles of cheese, black olives, strips of red peppers, and cubes of ham. Simpler breads are commonly dipped in a dish of mixed powdered spices called *ciubritsa* after its main ingredient, a spice similar to tarragon. *Banitsa* is a strudellike pastry made into pies filled with spinach, pumpkin, or sirene cheese. And in the late summer, the making of *slivova*, or plum brandy, is an event that involves the entire community in every step of the process, from the bringing of baskets full of plums to the still to the joyous celebration when the first batch is tasted. Today, Bulgarian-American communities continue to enjoy these traditional foods at church and family feasts and celebrations.

This young parishioner at St. Cyril and St. Methody Bulgarian Orthodox Church in Granite City, Illinois, poses with a lapful of pastry while taking part in the celebration held in honor of the consecration of the new church building there in the late 1980s.

This 1951 pencil-and-sepia drawing by the Bulgarian-American artist Christo, entitled Factory in Plovdiv, Bulgaria, *depicts the interior of his father's textile factory.*

SUCCESS IN THE NEW WORLD

For many reasons, it is difficult to write about today's Bulgarian-American community. The most significant is its size, or lack thereof. Even at their greatest numbers in the New World, the Bulgarians constituted one of the smallest immigrant groups. Their geographic dispersal across the North American continent further diluted the Bulgarian influence, as did the return of many immigrants to the homeland once they had earned sufficent money. Today, after decades of assimilation, the problem is even more difficult. In some ways, the invisibility of the Bulgarian Americans is a testimony to the success of their efforts at assimilation. Nikolay Altankov, author of one of the few comprehensive analyses of Bulgarian Americans, has written that in comparison with other minority groups, the Bulgarians "are certainly much less conspicuous in the public eye, tending to keep their own affairs to themselves and to avoid involvement in American public life." Nevertheless, some Bulgarians have achieved noteworthy public attention; the great majority of others can boast of private triumphs, both in terms of overcoming great obstacles to build a new life in North America and in the success of their children and descendants.

Author and Politician

Stoyan Christowe was born in a small Macedonian village in 1897. In 1912, at the age of 15, he came to America with an uncle and several men from his village. After a difficult journey on foot, donkey, train, and steamship, Christowe and his companions reached North America. In his autobiographical novel, entitled *This Is My Country* and published in 1938, Christowe described his first view of America:

> The next morning, after a hurried breakfast, I ran up on deck. I was one of the first there. The *Oceanic* seemed to have sailed into some kind of lake, for all around sprawled the New World. Directly in front, rising precipitously out of the water, was a pile of buildings clustered together and rearing up in serried terraces. Some of them had flat tops, others were surmounted by cupolas and slender towers, and the whole group reminded me of prints of Jerusalem I had seen in the old country. To the left from an island, rose a great statue, representing a human form, with its right arm uplifted like the sole branch of a giant tree. I had seen monuments in some European cities where we had waited for trains, but I had seen nothing to compare with this in size. Somehow it occurred to me that such a colossal statue placed at the threshold of America must have some special significance.

After passing inspection at Ellis Island, Christowe traveled to St. Louis, where other men of his village had settled. These friends found him a job in a locomotive factory, but the noise, filth, and strangeness of the plant distressed him. He left the job on his first day and found another making shoes.

Christowe soon found the shoe factory dull and the Bulgarian ghetto depressing. Most Macedonian and Bulgarian immigrants kept themselves apart and

Longtime Vermont state senator and critically acclaimed writer Stoyan Christowe came to America in 1912. His three volumes of memoirs constitute one of the finest literary evocations of the Bulgarian-American experience.

resisted assimilation; they had come to America only to earn the money that would make life comfortable for their families when they returned to Bulgaria. But the 15-year-old Christowe wanted to experience life in America; he regarded his fellow countrymen as mere sojourners, uninterested in the new life around them.

Soon, Christowe was offered the opportunity to work on the railroads in Montana. The pay was good, the company covered living expenses, and the job allowed Christowe to escape the St. Louis ghetto. When the weather was warm, the crew built and repaired the tracks of the Great Northern Railroad. In cold weather, Christowe spent most of his time studying English in the boxcar he had been given as living quarters. After two years of this spartan existence, Christowe had learned the language well enough to qualify for entrance to Valparaiso University in Indiana. After graduation, Christowe spent a year in Chicago, pondering his future and writing articles for magazines and newspapers. In 1928, he spent a year in the Balkans as a special correspondent for the Chicago *Daily News*.

While visiting his homeland, Christowe noted that although he wrote about "donkeys and storks, dancing bears, gypsies baking bread," the real drama of the Balkans lay in its long history of violence, oppression, and poverty. As a visitor with a pocketful of American money, Christowe observed that "in Bulgaria everything was delightful and easy for me compared to my struggles and hardships in the United States." Christowe journeyed to the town he had left as a 15 year old and observed the men who had emigrated and later returned to their homeland:

> I saw men in native garb but with an odd piece of clothing, such as a vest or a jacket, or a felt hat the worse for wear, or even a pair of shoes that bespoke America. I know they had at some time in their lives been in America and had returned here to goad donkeys, to replant themselves in their earth, from which they had really never transplanted themselves even while they were in America.

In 1961, Christowe was elected to the Vermont state senate. He has written several books, including memoirs, novels, and a study of Macedonian revolutionaries. Christowe's thoughts on assimilation are in many ways illustrative of the immigrant experience: "You cannot hide from your people. In fact the smaller the nation of which you are a member the harder it is for you to lose yourself in another world. Especially if you have distinguished yourself in the smallest degree you will be tracked down and reminded of your roots and antecedents. You cannot entirely escape your birthright even though you have gone through ten Americanization processes."

Artist and Iconoclast

Christo is one of today's most controversial artists. His work has been both praised and ridiculed throughout the art world, although his work is rarely mentioned in Bulgaria. Christo Javacheff was born in 1935 in Gabrovo, Bulgaria. After years in Prague, Vienna, and Paris, he and Jeanne-Claude Christo Javacheff, née de Guillebon, his wife and collaborator, settled in New York in 1964 with their son, Cyril. [The material in this section is derived from an interview the authors conducted with Christo in March of 1988. Quoted material is taken verbatim from that conversation.]

By that time, Christo's work had long drawn the attention of those interested in nontraditional art forms. In Paris in 1958, Christo had begun wrapping small objects, as well as furniture and a car, using resin-steeped cloth and string for some of the projects. In the early 1960s, he experimented with wrapping the living human form. Christo raised the ire of the Parisians

Portrait of the artist as a young man: Christo Javacheff (left), his mother Tzveta Javacheva, and his older brother Anani Javacheff were photographed in Varna, a Bulgarian summer resort on the Black Sea, in 1939 or 1940. Christo credits his mother with steering him toward a career in art.

when he blocked off the rue Visconti for 3 hours with an "iron curtain" consisting of 204 stacked oil drums. The project was Christo's comment on the first anniversary of the construction of the Berlin Wall. He considers his work "public art" and believes that "any work of art is in a sense social comment."

Once in America, Christo was free to embark on even more monumental projects. In 1972, he created the orange *Valley Curtain*. Measuring 365 feet high and 1,368 feet across at its tallest and widest points, requiring 200,000 square feet of fabric, 110,000 pounds of steel cables, and 800 tons of concrete, *Valley Curtain* billowed across an area of the Grand Hogback Mountains in Rifle, Colorado, for 28 hours before a storm forced Christo to dismantle it.

In 1976, Christo completed *Running Fence*, 2 million square feet of white fabric 18 feet high that snaked over more than 24 miles of California's hilly Sonoma and Marin counties. In 1985, Christo created *The Pont Neuf Wrapped* by wrapping the oldest bridge in Paris with 440,000 square feet of fabric and 42,900 feet of rope. Perhaps Christo's most spectacular project was 1983's *Surrounded Islands*, which involved surrounding the perimeters of 11 small islands in Biscayne Bay, Florida, with a total of 6.5 million square feet of hot pink floating fabric.

Although Christo's works are not permanent, each requires years of preparation. The artist must win the support of reluctant officials and outraged citizens, out-wait an often slow-moving bureaucracy, and work with engineers to overcome the physical problems of each site. Christo calls the planning stage of a work the "software" and the implementation of the work the "hardware."

Currently, Christo is working on a joint Japanese and American project called the *The Umbrellas*, a project that will emphasize the similarities and differences in the roads, villages, and riverbanks of the area 72 miles north of Tokyo and of that 60 miles north of Los Angeles.

Another work, *Wrapped Reichstag, Project for Berlin*, involves the wrapping of Germany's former parliament building. Christo envisions a project for Central Park in New York called *The Gates*, the fabric of which "will underline the organic design in contrast to the geometric grid pattern of Manhattan and will harmonize with the beauty of Central Park." A monumental structure of stacked oil drums, to be called *The Mastaba of Abu Dhabi, Project for the United Arab Emirates*, will serve as a "symbol of [the] civilization of oil throughout the world."

Christo's earliest memories date from the time he was seven years old and American airplanes bombarded Bulgaria, Germany's ally in World War II. Christo's father was a chemist who owned a lab adjacent to his own textile factory. When the war ended, Bulgaria's newly formed Communist government nationalized all private businesses, including his father's

Workers erect a section of Christo's conceptual piece Running Fence *north of Petaluma, California, in September 1976. The 18-foot-high nylon fence ran for 24 miles over hills and through farms, ending at the Pacific Ocean.*

factory. Throughout Bulgaria and the other Soviet satellite countries, Stalin's followers began to persecute anyone who was suspected of harboring anti-Communist ideas. Christo remembers that "there was hunting of all the enemies of the people, and my father was accused by the state of sabotaging some of the laboratories. He was taken to prison. On our walls it was written 'Here lives an enemy of the people.'" The authorities arrested and imprisoned Christo's father in early 1948, but he was released in 1951 because the Bulgarian government required his talents as a scientist. The family then relocated to Plovdiv, the second largest city in Bulgaria, where Christo attended the gymnasium, or high school.

Christo's mother, Tzveta Javacheva, was a profound influence on his artistic career. In the 1920s she was the executive secretary of the Fine Arts Academy in Sofia; throughout the Second World War, writers, painters, and architects gathered in the family's home. It was she who hired a tutor to give her promising son lessons in "geometry, architecture, drawing, painting, the history of art and sculpture" and was responsible for his "continuous training in the relationships of art," training that began for the young boy at the age of six.

When he was 17, Christo began study at the Fine Arts Academy in Sofia. During the summers, he was required to attend a military camp, as all young Bulgarian men were required to serve in the armed forces. Christo remembers that the school itself was run on "a very stiff educational system" based on "social realism with an extremely academic program. In some ways [it was] very conservative and in some ways very interesting. For example, we had four semesters of medicine, and we studied the dissection of the human body in a medical school. This was art school based in the 19th century." Although he disliked his studies, Christo admits that "in the end it was all very interesting that we got through that. Of course we had all this Marxist education . . . very strict."

Because the academy censored art books, its students were deprived of knowledge of some of the 20th century's most exciting artists. Christo remembers that "it was as if Picasso, Braque, Klee never existed." However, several of the professors had emigrated from Russia in the 1920s, and they brought with them stories about the fascinating pre-Stalin Russian art world. From them Christo learned that creative artists "did a variety of contemporary art" in public places such as railway stations "to explore dynamics of art outside of the privileged museum world . . . to see that art should be subversive and should go beyond commodity and the object."

On weekends the students were sent to beautify the land around the railroad tracks of the Orient Express, which sliced through 720 miles of Bulgaria. Such beautification projects were intended to convince the railway's western passengers that the Communist government had succeeded in its promise of raising Bulgaria's standard of living. Christo recalls:

> Basically what we were doing was telling the farmers where to park their combines near the tracks or how to stack their hay up on the hill so it would be visible and there would be no mess around the railway tracks. Certainly this developed my later interest in communicating, discussing, and talking to people outside of the academic world. Also I started to learn the physicality of one kilometer, a hundred meters distance, topography, space and so on.

In 1956, Christo applied for permission to visit an uncle in Prague, Czechoslovakia. Prague was a more westernized city than Sofia, and the critical and outspoken Christo felt that there he would have a greater opportunity to pursue his work. "Impatient to get there, I borrowed the money to go by plane. Three days after I arrived in Czechoslovakia the revolution broke out in

Hungary, causing turmoil in all the Communist countries. The Soviets crushed the rebellion." Christo decided not to return to Bulgaria, even though by doing so he would be considered a deserter from the military:

> Every day people were escaping to the West. I had my chance to escape to Vienna. With the help of a doctor, a few families and I hid in a sealed railway car that was taking medical supplies to Vienna. We paid customs officials not to betray us to the police.

Christo knew that once arrived in Vienna he was required to go to a refugee camp. Not wanting to risk being confined for months, he abandoned his suitcase (so as not to look like a refugee) and took a cab to the home of an old friend of his father's. The following day, Christo registered at the Vienna Fine Arts Academy. With his student card, he was able to renounce his Bulgarian citizenship and became a political refugee.

After a semester in Vienna and six months in Geneva, Switzerland, in 1958 Christo went to Paris, where he began to develop his own distinctive artistic style. He supported himself by painting portraits of the well-to-do, which is how he met his wife, Jeanne-Claude.

Unfortunately, as has been true for many of the Bulgarian exiles who have come to America since World War II, his escape from Bulgaria had negative repercussions for his family. "Of course, I was a deserter. It was very complicated and made things worse for my parents. For a long time I didn't have any communication with my parents or relatives, except for letters, until Carter's administration in 1976. It was a difficult time." The only information the family could get was from occasional Bulgarian news articles that quoted stories from the Soviet press. These stories generally reduced Christo's work to artistic manifestations of "capitalism and imperial elitism." When his father was finally allowed to visit him in 1976, Christo learned that Bul-

Christo poses in his studio in front of drawings and sketches of some of his works, including The Pont Neuf Wrapped.

garians were virtually unaware of his projects. His art remains a bold challenge to social authority and artistic tradition, an iconoclasm he credits in no small part to his heritage:

> I am half Macedonian. Yes, the Macedonians are professional revolutionaries you know, they're really professional terrorists. I must say . . . they're an extremely independent and subversive people.

Exploring the Mind

Psychiatrist George Kamen has lived a modest life in New York City since his arrival in 1980. Occasionally he is asked why he abandoned a position of esteem, professional renown, and privilege in Bulgaria for a private life in America. For Kamen there is only one answer: the desire for freedom. [The material in this section is derived from an interview the authors conducted with George Kamen in July of 1989. Quoted material is taken verbatim from that conversation.]

Kamen was born in 1942, the son of a lawyer and a housewife. He remembers well how in the aftermath of World War II the Bulgarian government began to round up citizens suspected of being anti-Communists. "I remember how people disappeared, neighbors, schoolmates, in the fifties. We were taught that we should spy on our parents. Our parents could be enemies of the people. We would have to tell the teacher."

Even as a young boy, Kamen dreamed of emigrating. A Belgian-born friend of his mother's fascinated him with her talk of France and of French culture. His father insisted that he learn the German language. Both experiences provided him a glimpse of life outside of Bulgaria. While attending medical school in Sofia with the intention of becoming a psychiatrist, Kamen gained access to much new information about the West. He wrote to psychiatrists in West Germany and read newspapers, magazines, and books. "My idea was, after I graduated, I would escape the country. I was making plans even as a young man."

Upon graduating from medical school, Kamen became a member of the Bulgarian Medical Academy as a lecturer in the department of psychiatry. His election to the academy was somewhat unusual and indicative of the lack of freedom Kamen would come to find so confining. In the Bulgarian medical system, a three-year assigned residency, usually in one's hometown, is mandatory; after the three years, a doctor is allowed to choose where he or she would like to work, but to move from one city to another, police approval is required. In order to take a post at the academy in Sofia, Kamen was required to take a competitive exam. Although his performance was considered superior to that of the other students, the permanent post was awarded to a young doctor from the Soviet Union whose father was a prominent political figure in Bulgaria. In order to retain Kamen as well, the academy's commission requested a temporary position for him. Later, the awarding of that special position was used to manipulate Kamen. The authorities could extend or cut short the expiration of Kamen's official permission to remain in Sofia as they saw fit; Kamen, as the recipient of a special favor, was not in a position to argue their decision.

Kamen was drawn to the works of Freud and Jung, as well as to the idea of group therapy. "I started pretty early, right after I started my residency. I began experimenting with group therapy in 1968. Then, in 1969–70, I wrote a letter to a very prominent group therapist in Switzerland; he encouraged me."

In 1973, Kamen wrote an article that presented group therapy to the Bulgarians for the first time. The article was published in a heavily edited version and severely criticized. Undeterred, Kamen began to lead group therapy sessions after his usual day's work. "Then the government and medical authorities slowly started getting interested, and I was allowed to do things which, in the beginning, I didn't think they would let me do."

Kamen continued the sessions during work hours, expanded his therapy groups, and wrote additional articles that were published in West Germany, Switzerland, and the United States, despite the Bulgarian government's official disapproval. The government's regard for him as a "national treasure" prevented Kamen's leaving the Eastern bloc for any reason, private or professional, although he was allowed to attend a few international meetings in Eastern Europe. Kamen was catapulted into national fame when a filmmaker decided to make a movie based on his work:

> In Bulgaria, they showed a limited audience *One Flew Over the Cuckoo's Nest*, and one of the Bulgarian producers was very impressed and wanted to make something similar. He started with the head of my department, and then we met. He decided the main character would be somebody who would play me.

Although the movie was shown in Bulgaria only after Kamen's departure, his new popularity with government officials proved unfortunate. They began to see ways in which his work could be used to their advantage. Kamen was ordered to report to the authorities any potentially political information his patients revealed. One patient mentioned that a relative had escaped to the West and had urged her to escape as well. Kamen remembers that he was "frightened to death because I knew I should report that to the police. I didn't know if the patient was an agent just trying to see if I was loyal enough. I could go to jail for knowing something like that." Not long afterward Kamen was turned down for a promotion, ostensibly because he was not sufficiently loyal to the Bulgarian government.

The introduction of group therapy into a Communist society was a daring, dangerous, and potentially liberating step. Hypnosis, the more favored form of therapeutic treatment, was often used to indoctrinate the patient into one system of thought, but group therapy encouraged the patient to express his or her unique thoughts and emotions. Over time, Kamen's patients began to question the structure of their lives under the repressive Bulgarian government. Frustrated by the possession of new knowledge and the lack of opportunities in which to use and benefit from that insight, Kamen's patients were in some ways more troubled than they had been prior to their therapy. Caught between harassment by the authorities and the ultimate failure of group therapy in a socialist system, Kamen determined to leave Bulgaria.

Naturally a cautious man, Kamen did not want to risk a dangerous escape that might result in his capture. He first attempted to escape through Yugoslavia, but the contact scheduled to lead him through the mountains, ostensibly as a sort of excursion guide, did not show. Unused to mountain travel, Kamen could not proceed on foot and had to turn back. His next attempt involved a West German friend driving across the Yugoslavian border, at a location where cars were not frequently searched, with Kamen hidden in the car. Unfortunately, Kamen's friend started shaking badly as they approached the guards, and the attempt was abandoned. A third attempt also ended in failure when a truck driver who Kamen had helped avoid severe punishment for having criticized the Bulgarian president failed to show.

Kamen began to be harassed by unknown tormenters. Attempts were made to break into his apartment, and stones were thrown at the windows. When Kamen reported the incidents to the police, he was told that the assailants were his "crazy" patients. One morning he found a makeshift grave and cross by his door. The harassment continued nightly for a month. Kamen began to receive anonymous phone calls that warned of his death if he did not "get out." The phone company agreed to trace the calls but then denied his ever having received them.

Kamen gambled on escape one final time. Friends in West Germany arranged an invitation for him to attend

Dr. George Kamen and his son George, Jr., enjoy a warm and sunny day in New York City. For the elder Kamen, the freedom to be found in the West was worth relinquishing personal and professional renown.

a conference in Austria. When an exit visa was denied, other friends managed to steal his passport from the Department of Health. Kamen bought a ticket to Vienna, a return ticket to Bulgaria, and took his chances. As his passport was checked at the airport, he was strip-searched in an allegedly routine check for smuggled currency—a common method used by the authorities to humiliate and intimidate. He feared his motive for leaving had been found out, but he was allowed to continue on his way. In his great relief at being let go, he could not control hysterical laughter.

From Vienna, Kamen made his way to West Germany, where he asked for political asylum. He began to correspond secretly, through a post office box, with Katia Bogdanova, a woman he had met in Bulgaria shortly before his escape. Meanwhile, having discovered him missing, the Bulgarian authorities falsely announced that Kamen was in West Germany on a business trip and spread a rumor that he was a high-ranking spy. Through a friendly connection, Katia learned that the Bulgarian government was secretly planning to kidnap Kamen and spirit him across the West German border into Communist East Germany. Katia, who at the time was in Morocco with a Bulgarian company, asked to return to Bulgaria but instead made her way to Germany, where she and Kamen married. Kamen was not retaken by the Bulgarian government.

In 1980 the Kamens moved to Chicago. Kamen decided to start afresh. It was an "experiment, it worked. I had to face misery, poverty . . . all those kind of survival things. Many people cannot understand why I left a high position in Bulgaria, a high position in Germany. I came here and struggled with life. Some people think I'm crazy. When we went back to Germany years later, we had the feeling that everything was frozen just the way we left it. We said, thank God at least our life is interesting."

Kamen now has a private practice in Manhattan and treats patients using techniques of Freudian psycho-analysis. He and his wife have become involved in Radio Free Europe, with Katia serving as the coordinator of a program called "U.S. Life and Society." Kamen put together a general medical show featuring topics in psychiatry, on which he presented both the benefits and the risks of advanced medical technology.

His radio broadcasts have yielded benefits for Kamen. Because as a result of the programs the Bulgarian government now considers him an expert on Western medicine, it has allowed family members to visit him. It has even recently issued an official invitation for him to participate in a meeting of Bulgaria's Department of Health, but Kamen, at least prior to the fall of the Zhivkov regime, has always refused to return. He loves living in New York City and having the freedom to do the work he had always hoped to do without jeopardizing his career or his family.

Conclusion

Today, the sense of Bulgarian ethnicity is strongest among those Bulgarian Americans who have remained active in the Bulgarian Orthodox church and who have maintained close family ties. But traditional tightly knit patriarchal families have grown less common among the second and third generations of Bulgarian Americans, and those Bulgarians who have emigrated to the United States since Bulgaria became a Communist state are less likely to seek out the older, church-centered Bulgarian-American communities. This later group coordinated the institution of several anti-Communist and nationalistic organizations in America, including the Bulgarian National Front, Inc. (founded in 1948), and the Bulgarian National Committee (founded in 1949). Today, to an extent unknown among earlier generations, Bulgarian Americans are beginning to exhibit an interest in American local and national politics and to seek political representation. In 1975, Democrat Ivan Lebamov, mayor of Fort Wayne, Indiana, designated Plovdiv, Bulgaria, as Fort Wayne's sister city, an indication that although today's Bulgarian Americans are thoroughly assimilated, they still possess a great deal of ethnic awareness and pride.

Many Bulgarian Americans have successfully established small businesses, such as restaurants, taverns, grocery stores, bakeries, and construction companies. Since the end of World War II, the majority of Bulgarian immigrants have been professionals, such as doctors, architects, and engineers, frustrated by the restrictions placed on them under communism. Most Bulgarian

Americans live and work in urban centers. The largest concentration of Bulgarian Americans, numbering 10,000, live in Michigan, with smaller communities in Ohio, Indiana, Illinois, New York, New Jersey, Pennsylvania, Missouri, and California. The cities with the greatest concentration of Bulgarian Americans are Detroit, Michigan; Gary, Fort Wayne, and Indianapolis, Indiana; Lorain, Toledo, Cleveland, Youngstown, and Akron, Ohio; New York City, New York; and Los Angeles, California. Pittsburgh, once the home of a significant Bulgarian-American community, has declined in prominence. Many of the more recent immigrants settle first in New York or Chicago and then head for Los Angeles. The majority of these individuals are well educated, enthusiastic, and young and have little difficulty adjusting to their new home.

Interest in such traditional facets of the immigrant community as fraternal organizations and in Slavic-language publications has declined as the first generation of immigrants ages and dies and succeeding generations learn English as their primary language and achieve economic and professional success. As has been true of the second generation of most immigrant groups, the sons and daughters of Bulgarian immigrants were eager to become Americanized and to shed the "differentness" that hindered their parents' progress. Nevertheless, this generation retained a respect for family and heritage. Members of the third generation, secure in their sense of themselves as Americans, generally exhibit a greater interest in their Bulgarian heritage than do their parents.

Nikolay Altankov notes that the success of the Bulgarian immigrant in retaining his ethnic identity and in becoming a successful member of the American community is remarkable considering his initial disadvantages. More than 90 percent of Bulgarian immigrants in the early years of the century were laborers with little money and little or no education. The number of Bulgarian immigrants was always small

and scattered geographically. The establishment of true communities was not possible at first because of the absence of families and because a significant number of men chose to repatriate before marrying. Nevertheless, such time-honored Bulgarian virtues as thrift, respect for hard work, and the desire for freedom enabled Bulgarians to make important contributions to American life. It is possible that with the easing of travel restrictions between East and West that has accompanied the lessening of cold war political tensions, America will soon be welcoming a new generation of Bulgarian immigrants. If so, there is every reason to believe they will exhibit the same qualities of courage, endurance, and ingenuity that distinguished their predecessors.

This statue of Januarius MacGahan was unveiled in 1984 in his hometown of New Lexington, Ohio, where the local Bulgarian-American community sponsors an annual festival in honor of MacGahan's birthday. The statue of the Bulgarian liberator stands as testimony to the continued links between Bulgaria and America.

FURTHER READING

Agneros, Jack, et al. *The Immigrant Experience, the Anguish of Becoming American.* New York: Dial Press, 1971.

Altankov, Nikolay G. *The Bulgarian-Americans.* Palo Alto, CA: Ragusan Press, 1979.

Appel, John J. ed. *The New Immigration.* New York: Pitman Ozar Books, 1971.

Byington, Margaret. *Homestead, the Households of a Mill Town.* 1910. Reprint. Pittsburgh: University Center for International Studies, 1974.

Christowe, Stoyan. *The Eagle and the Stork, an American Memoir.* New York: Harper's Magazine Press, 1976.

Dery, Mark. "Bulgarian Rhapsody: The Haunting Harmonies of Bulgaria Are Electrifying the Music World." *Elle*, March 1989.

Kramer, Jane. "Letter from Europe: Christo and Greenpeace Affair." *New Yorker*, October 21, 1985.

Life. "Covered Bridge, Pont Neuf Wrapped by Christo." November 1985.

Petroff, Boris George. *Son of the Danube.* New York: Viking, 1940.

Pribichevich, Stoyan. *Macedonia: Its People and History.* Pennsylvania State University Press, 1982.

Tamir, Vicki. *Bulgaria and Her Jews: The History of a Dubious Symbiosis.* New York: Sepher-Hermon Press for Yeshiva University Press, 1979.

Vazov, Ivan. *Under the Yoke.* New York: Twayne, 1971.

Yankoff, Peter D. *Peter Menikoff: The Story of a Bulgarian Boy in the Great American Melting Pot.* Nashville: Cokesbury Press, 1928.

INDEX

Ottoman Empire, 26–27, 29, 30, 31, 32, 41

Patriarch, 22, 27, 29, 30
Peter, czar of Bulgaria, 24
Peter Menikoff: The Story of a Bulgarian Boy in the Great American Melting Pot (Yankoff), 44–45, 48, 85
Petroff, Boris George, 85
Poptomov, V. I., 60
Prairie Mosaic: An Ethnic Atlas of Rural North Dakota (Sherman), 52
Protestant church, 46, 57

Quintet of Cuisines, A (Field and Field), 85

Roman Catholic church, 22
Romania, 13, 26, 31, 35, 45
Russia, 26, 29, 30, 31, 33, 37, 39, 40, 41, 45, 52

St. Cyril, 22, 23
St. Ilya's Day uprising, 16, 34
St. Methodius, 22, 23
Samuel, 24
Serbia, 16, 26, 34, 35
Sherman, William C., 52
Simeon, 24
Slavonic-Bulgarian History of the Peoples, Tsars and Saints, and of all their Deeds and of the Bulgarian Way of Life, A (Hilendnarski), 28

Sofia, Bulgaria, 13, 25, 41, 59, 60
Sofia Conservatory, 84
Son of the Danube (Petroff), 85
Stambulov, Stefan, 34
Strossmayer, Josip J., 29–30
Subranie, 33
Svyatoslav I, grand prince of Kiev, 24
Syoboda, 60

Teofilakt, Ieromanach, 60
This Is My Country (Christowe), 46, 90
Treaty of San Stefano, 32–33
Turkey, 13, 16, 26–27, 29, 35

Under the Yoke (Vazov), 85
Union of the Macedonian Political Organizations, 61

Vazov, Ivan, 84–85
Velichki, Andrei, 60
Vienna, Austria, 30, 48
Vienna State Opera, 84

Warsaw Pact, 40, 41
World War I, 16, 17, 36, 59
World War II, 19, 36–38, 41, 57, 95, 96, 99, 105

Yankoff, Peter, 44, 48, 49, 85
Yugoslavia, 13, 16

Zhivkov, Todor, 40, 41
Zimisces, John I., Byzantine emperor, 24
Zveno, 36–37

PICTURE CREDITS

CLAUDIA CARLSON, a professional writer and illustrator, received her B.A. in English at the State University of New York at Stony Brook. Her husband, DAVID ALLEN, earned his B.A. in history, also at SUNY at Stony Brook, and is the bookstore manager at Fordham University. Carlson and Allen live in New York City.

DANIEL PATRICK MOYNIHAN is the senior United States senator from New York. He is also the only person in American history to serve in the cabinets or subcabinets of four successive presidents—Kennedy, Johnson, Nixon, and Ford. Formerly a professor of government at Harvard University, he has written and edited many books, including *Beyond the Melting Pot*, *Ethnicity: Theory and Experience* (both with Nathan Glazer), *Loyalties*, and *Family and Nation*.